READINGS ON

THE OLD MAN AND THE SEA

OTHER TITLES IN THE GREENHAVEN PRESS LITERARY COMPANION SERIES:

AMERICAN AUTHORS

Maya Angelou
Stephen Crane
Emily Dickinson
William Faulkner
F. Scott Fitzgerald
Nathaniel Hawthorne
Ernest Hemingway
Herman Melville
Arthur Miller
Eugene O'Neill
Edgar Allan Poe
John Steinbeck
Mark Twain
Thornton Wilder

AMERICAN LITERATURE

The Adventures of
  Huckleberry Finn
The Adventures of Tom
  Sawyer
The Call of the Wild
The Catcher in the Rye
The Crucible
Death of a Salesman
The Glass Menagerie
The Grapes of Wrath
The Great Gatsby
Of Mice and Men
The Old Man and the Sea
The Pearl
The Scarlet Letter
A Separate Peace

BRITISH AUTHORS

Jane Austen
Joseph Conrad
Charles Dickens

BRITISH LITERATURE

Animal Farm
The Canterbury Tales
Great Expectations
Hamlet
Julius Caesar
Lord of the Flies
Macbeth
Pride and Prejudice
Romeo and Juliet
Shakespeare: The Comedies
Shakespeare: The Histories
Shakespeare: The Sonnets
Shakespeare: The Tragedies
A Tale of Two Cities
Wuthering Heights

WORLD AUTHORS

Fyodor Dostoyevsky
Homer
Sophocles

WORLD LITERATURE

All Quiet on the Western
  Front
The Diary of a Young Girl
A Doll's House

THE GREENHAVEN PRESS
Literary Companion
TO AMERICAN LITERATURE

READINGS ON

THE OLD MAN AND THE SEA

Bonnie Szumski, *Book Editor*

David L. Bender, *Publisher*
Bruno Leone, *Executive Editor*
Bonnie Szumski, *Series Editor*

Greenhaven Press, Inc., San Diego, CA

Every effort has been made to trace the owners of copy-righted material. The articles in this volume may have been edited for content, length, and/or reading level. The titles have been changed to enhance the editorial purpose. Those interested in locating the original source will find the complete citation on the first page of each article.

Library of Congress Cataloging-in-Publication Data

Readings on The old man and the sea / Bonnie Szumski [editor].
    p.   cm. — (The Greenhaven Press literary companion to American literature)
    Includes bibliographical references and index.
    ISBN 1-56510-843-4 (lib. : alk. paper). —
ISBN 1-56510-842-6 (pbk. : alk. paper)
    1. Hemingway, Ernest, 1899–1961. Old man and the sea. 2. Fishing stories, American—History and criticism. 3. Fables, American—History and criticism. 4. Aged men in literature. 5. Old age in literature. I. Szumski, Bonnie, 1958–   . II. Series.
PS3515.E370529   1999
813'.52—dc21   98-26704
                                                CIP

Cover photo: Photofest

Copyright ©1999 by Greenhaven Press, Inc.
PO Box 289009
San Diego, CA 92198-9009
Printed in the U.S.A.

> **"**I tried to make a real old man, a real boy, a real sea and a real fish and real shark, but if I make them good and true enough they would mean many things. The hardest thing is to make something really true and sometimes truer than true. **"**

Ernest Hemingway, 1954

CONTENTS

Foreword   9

Introduction   11

Ernest Hemingway: A Biography   13

Chapter 1: Themes in *The Old Man and the Sea*

1. ***The Old Man and the Sea* as Fable**
   by Delbert E. Wylder   32
   The Old Man and the Sea is written as a fable, with an archetypal journey that is larger than life. Yet the ending, which
   has elements of both defeat and victory, remains ambiguous.

2. ***The Old Man and the Sea* Is an Allegory
   of the Artist** *by Wirt Williams*   42
   The Old Man and the Sea is a simple allegory of the artist,
   represented by the old man, and the artist's creation, represented by the fish.

3. **Aging in *The Old Man and the Sea***
   by Stanley Cooperman   52
   Old age was not a favorite topic of Hemingway, whose heroes were required to maintain a virile, youthful stoicism.
   In *The Old Man and the Sea*, age is portrayed somewhat
   unrealistically.

4. ***The Old Man and the Sea* Is a Love Story**
   by Linda W. Wagner   59
   The relationship between Manolin and the old man is one
   of the most loving and realistic in all of Hemingway.

5. **Hemingway's Battle with God** *by Ben Stoltzfus*   69
   The Old Man and the Sea presents two points of view: those
   of the omniscient narrator/Hemingway and the old man. In
   the novel, it is Hemingway who heightens the old man's
   struggle with the marlin into a battle with God.

Chapter 2: The Novel's Artistic Accomplishment

1. **Excerpt from** *A Reader's Guide to Ernest Hemingway* **by** *Arthur Waldhorn*   79
   Although many critics have found grander symbols and themes in *The Old Man and the Sea*, it works best when read as a straightforward, lyrical story.

2. **Symbolism in** *The Old Man and the Sea* **by** *Keiichi Harada*   88
   Although *The Old Man and the Sea* is very successful as a straightforward story, symbol and allegory make it an even greater accomplishment.

3. **Hemingway's Religious Symbolism** *by Joseph Waldmeir*   96
   Hemingway's religious symbolism is not meant to link Santiago with Christ. Hemingway rather openly dismisses religion in favor of man's involvement in the natural world.

4. **Biblical Allusions in** *The Old Man and the Sea* **by** *Joseph M. Flora*   104
   Hemingway uses several key events in the Bible to point out a basic theme: the old man adheres to the value system of Christianity.

5. **A Lack of Realism Mars** *The Old Man and the Sea* **by** *Robert P. Weeks*   109
   Unbelievable coincidences and exaggerations make *The Old Man and the Sea* a flawed, tedious work. Hemingway is at his best when he writes of what he knows, and this novel, while good, is second-rate.

Chapter 3: The Character of the Old Man

1. **The Old Man Maintains a Fighting Code** *by Wolfgang Wittkowski*   118
   The old man is a typical Hemingway figure, attempting to transcend his animal nature by participating in a grand fight, in this case, against the elements of nature.

2. **The Old Man Is a Spiritual Figure** *by William J. Handy*   128
   Although an unsuccessful fisherman, the old man remains sanguine about his circumstances. He is concerned not with practical materialism, but rather with a grander, spiritual existence.

3. **The Old Man's Classic Quest** *by Robert O. Stephens* 139
In pursuing the marlin, the old man participates in the archetypal quest for spiritual enlightenment. *The Old Man
and the Sea* is reminiscent of *Moby-Dick* and other great
sea stories that attempt the same juxtaposition.

4. **The Old Man's Heroic Struggle** *by Leo Gurko* 147
Because the old man is not permanently wounded or disillusioned, he is to Hemingway a heroic figure.

5. **The Old Man Is Not a Heroic Figure**
by Chaman Nahal 157
The Old Man and the Sea is a tale of hopeless resignation,
not of heroic struggle. It is in Santiago's passive acceptance
of his fate that he achieves nobility.

Chronology 165

For Further Research 169

Works by Ernest Hemingway 172

Index 173

FOREWORD

*"'Tis the good reader that
makes the good book."*

Ralph Waldo Emerson

The story's bare facts are simple: The captain, an old and scarred seafarer, walks with a peg leg made of whale ivory. He relentlessly drives his crew to hunt the world's oceans for the great white whale that crippled him. After a long search, the ship encounters the whale and a fierce battle ensues. Finally the captain drives his harpoon into the whale, but the harpoon line catches the captain about the neck and drags him to his death.

A simple story, a straightforward plot—yet, since the 1851 publication of Herman Melville's *Moby-Dick*, readers and critics have found many meanings in the struggle between Captain Ahab and the whale. To some, the novel is a cautionary tale that depicts how Ahab's obsession with revenge leads to his insanity and death. Others believe that the whale represents the unknowable secrets of the universe and that Ahab is a tragic hero who dares to challenge fate by attempting to discover this knowledge. Perhaps Melville intended Ahab as a criticism of Americans' tendency to become involved in well-intentioned but irrational causes. Or did Melville model Ahab after himself, letting his fictional character express his anger at what he perceived as a cruel and distant god?

Although literary critics disagree over the meaning of *Moby-Dick*, readers do not need to choose one particular interpretation in order to gain an understanding of Melville's

9

novel. Instead, by examining various analyses, they can gain numerous insights into the issues that lie under the surface of the basic plot. Studying the writings of literary critics can also aid readers in making their own assessments of *Moby-Dick* and other literary works and in developing analytical thinking skills.

The Greenhaven Literary Companion Series was created with these goals in mind. Designed for young adults, this unique anthology series provides an engaging and comprehensive introduction to literary analysis and criticism. The essays included in the Literary Companion Series are chosen for their accessibility to a young adult audience and are expertly edited in consideration of both the reading and comprehension levels of this audience. In addition, each essay is introduced by a concise summation that presents the contributing writer's main themes and insights. Every anthology in the Literary Companion Series contains a varied selection of critical essays that cover a wide time span and express diverse views. Wherever possible, primary sources are represented through excerpts from authors' notebooks, letters, and journals and through contemporary criticism.

Each title in the Literary Companion Series pays careful consideration to the historical context of the particular author or literary work. In-depth biographies and detailed chronologies reveal important aspects of authors' lives and emphasize the historical events and social milieu that influenced their writings. To facilitate further research, every anthology includes primary and secondary source bibliographies of articles and/or books selected for their suitability for young adults. These engaging features make the Greenhaven Literary Companion series ideal for introducing students to literary analysis in the classroom or as a library resource for young adults researching the world's great authors and literature.

Exceptional in its focus on young adults, the Greenhaven Literary Companion Series strives to present literary criticism in a compelling and accessible format. Every title in the series is intended to spark readers' interest in leading American and world authors, to help them broaden their understanding of literature, and to encourage them to formulate their own analyses of the literary works that they read. It is the editors' hope that young adult readers will find these anthologies to be true companions in their study of literature.

INTRODUCTION

Like his fictional old man, Hemingway fished the waters off Havana for marlin. While doing so, he developed a deep admiration for the Cuban fishermen who made their living in this way. In an essay "On the Blue Water: A Gulf Stream Letter" published in 1936 for *Esquire* magazine, Ernest Hemingway detailed a story about an old man who

> hooked a giant marlin that, on the heavy sashcord handline, pulled the skiff far out to sea. Two days later the old man was picked up by fishermen 60 miles to the eastward, the head and forward part of the marlin lashed alongside. What was left of this fish, less than half, weighed eight hundred pounds. The old man had stayed with him a day, a night, a day and another night while the fish swam deep and pulled the boat. When he had come up the old man had pulled the boat up on him and harpooned him. Lashed alongside the sharks had hit him and the old man had fought them out alone in the Gulf Stream in a skiff, clubbing them, stabbing at them, lunging at them with an oar until he was exhausted and the sharks had eaten all that they could hold. He was crying in the boat when the fishermen picked him up, half crazy from his loss, and the sharks were still circling the boat.

It would take Hemingway another fifteen years to transform the memory of this old man and his plight into the premise of his short novel *The Old Man and the Sea*. It was an instant success, and its simplicity has continued to enthrall readers.

The Old Man and the Sea's enduring qualities lie in its almost universal appeal. The main character, fighting age and a string of bad luck, goes off in deeper water only to find the ultimate fight with an enormous marlin. During the days it takes to reel in the marlin and kill it, as well as on the return journey and his fight with sharks to keep the fish intact, the old man's philosophical musings on the meaning of life and death, and his role in both, provide a fascinating backdrop for this straightforward tale.

In part because of its brevity, *The Old Man and the Sea* is the first Hemingway many readers encounter. In this Literary

Companion title, essayists probe the depths of the book's meaning to prove that the story is anything but one-dimensional. Whereas Melville's *Moby-Dick*, another sea tale, is rife with complexity, *The Old Man and the Sea* seems little more than a realistic, dramatic fish story. Yet, typical of Hemingway, the elegant simplicity belies deeper themes.

Readings on The Old Man and the Sea contains several helpful features for those new to literary criticism. Each essay's introduction summarizes the article's main ideas and gives a bit of background on the author. Notes explain difficult or unfamiliar words and concepts throughout the book. A chronology lists important dates in the life of the author presented in a broader historical context. A bibliography includes works for further research as well as historical works of interest. Finally, an annotated table of contents and thorough index make each volume in the Literary Companion Series a complete tool in itself as well as a launching point for further exploration.

ERNEST HEMINGWAY: A BIOGRAPHY

Ernest Hemingway gazes out from the covers of two hefty literary biographies. On one, a passport photo shows a young man in his late teens, intense, assertive, self-confident (a bit cocky?), clean-shaven, good-looking. On the other, a somewhat grizzled man of about sixty, gray hair and beard a bit shaggy, seems to be slightly confused, unsure of himself, vulnerable. The first photo is of a young man who had yet to make his mark; the second, the winner of numerous literary awards including the Pulitzer and Nobel prizes—the Grand Old Man of Literature—who would commit suicide not long after the photo was taken.

Taking his own life cast a long shadow back over Hemingway's accomplishments. Most literary (and personal) analyses since his death in 1961 have been colored by the fact of his self-destruction, and several biographers have tried to understand how that cocky young man, after achieving more than most men ever dream, became the unhappy man of his last years. Many find some of the seeds of sadness in the relationship between his mother and his father, and in his relationships with them.

GRACE AND CLARENCE HEMINGWAY

Grace Hall Hemingway, Ernest's mother, was the daughter and granddaughter of strong-willed women, and she was raised to think highly of herself. She had chafed under the restrictions placed on girls when she was growing up and had in fact been a bit of a tomboy. (She rode her brother's bicycle down the street, a caper considered shocking at the time.) Hemingway biographer Kenneth S. Lynn says she was a "gifted, charming, physically impressive woman." Trained for a career in music, she failed to become a premier soprano when she had a traumatic debut at New York City's Madison Square Garden in 1896. (The circumstances have been variously reported, but she apparently

13

was unable to perform under the bright lights of the stage.) Giving up her dream, as she put it, she consented to marry Clarence Hemingway, a young doctor who had helped treat her mother at home during her final illness.

The Hemingways lived near Chicago in Oak Park, Illinois, a community that considered itself above the norm according to such standards as culture and social caste. Grace had no problem beginning a second career there, earning her own money as a music teacher. (In the early years of their marriage, she made more than Clarence did.) In a society that was just beginning to consider women as no longer completely ruled by men (although women would still not be allowed to vote in national elections until 1920), Grace refused to play a traditional, subservient role. She ignored Clarence's edicts when she chose to; for example, she caused quite a strain in the relationship when she insisted on purchasing a second vacation home for her personal use near the family's longtime summer home in Michigan. (She once warned Ernest, after Clarence had died, "Never threaten me with what to do. Your father tried that once when we were first married and he lived to regret it.") Ernest and other family members remembered times when she had humiliated Clarence in public, which he seems generally to have taken in stoic silence. Grace also considered it beneath her to do the cooking and housework, so it frequently fell to her husband to tend to domestic life after he returned home from work. It seems likely that Clarence suffered from a form of depression, which may have made him less able to cope with such a relationship. At any rate, when Clarence committed suicide in 1928, Ernest blamed his mother.

"TWINS"

Grace and Clarence's first child, Marcelline, was born January 15, 1898. Oddly, after Ernest Miller Hemingway was born some eighteen months later, on July 21, 1899, Grace insisted on treating the two children as if they were twins. Ernest was often clothed in dresses like Marcelline's—a custom that was not too odd at the time. But his mother also occasionally referred to him as her "beautiful girl" or "summer girl."

Grace had Marcelline's schooling delayed so she and Ernest could enter school together, as the "twins" they were supposed to be. Since Marcelline was a year and a half older than her brother, she was more advanced both physically and intellectually during the several years they were schooled together. Treating Ernest and Marcelline alike may have been Grace's attempt to give her daughter the equality she had wanted for herself, but for Ernest it added a frustrating element to the inevitable sibling rivalry.

AN ORDINARY CHILDHOOD

Ernest would eventually have four sisters and a brother. The outer trappings of the Hemingway children's childhood were those of a fairly privileged middle-class family. Grace regularly took her children on culturally enriching treks to nearby Chicago. Summers were spent at Windemere, the family's cottage on Walloon Lake in Michigan, where Clarence shared with his son his considerable proficiency in fishing, hunting, and other outdoor skills.

Oak Park was a religious community, and the routine piety of the Hemingway family fitted the town's norm. Prayer and Bible readings were part of the Hemingways' daily routine, and a strict observance of rules both secular and religious was required. Drinking, like dancing, was a sin. Ernest seems to have been an obedient son for the most part, and a repentant one when he strayed.

Yet there were signs of the determinedly self-defined man he would become. Hemingway biographer Carlos Baker notes that Ernest learned to box in 1916; he adds, "There was a streak of the bully in his nature which began to emerge when he learned of the power in his fists." In 1940 his editor, Maxwell Perkins, related an anecdote in which he discerned Ernest's boyhood persistence and courage:

> One of the earliest stories significant of his character I do know to be fact. When he was still a boy, but large for his age and strong, his father, yielding to his urgency, gave him the price of an advertised course in boxing. You paid the ex-fighter in advance and he turned you over to a pug. In the first lesson young Hemingway got rough treatment. His nose was broken. Few returned for a second lesson, but Hemingway did, and he finished the course. It never even occurred to him that this was a racket—that you weren't supposed to come back ever.

That determination to face fear and pain found expression in Hemingway's "code of the hero." The code would become an important part of his writing, and of his life. So, to a lesser extent, would his tendency to be a bully.

JOURNALISM VS. WAR

A few months after he graduated from high school in June 1917, his uncle Alfred Tyler Hemingway helped him get a job as a cub reporter with the *Kansas City Star*. This seems to have been a compromise with his parents: they wanted him to go to college, and he wanted to volunteer to help fight the war against Germany. (The United States had just entered World War I in April of that year.)

Ernest spent several months at the *Star*, learning on the job about the newspaper trade. His boss, C.G. Wellington, gave him the newspaper's style sheet and told him to memorize—and apply—the long list of dos and don'ts: "Use short sentences. Use short first paragraphs. Use vigorous English. Be positive, not negative." He would later say these were "the best rules" he had ever learned for writing.

But he still wanted to go to war. By early 1918, when Italian Red Cross officials arrived in Kansas City on a recruitment drive, he was eager to sign up. (The Red Cross was only allowed to recruit men who could not be drafted; Hemingway had defective vision in his left eye.) When he was accepted, he gave his notice to the *Star*, leaving the paper at the end of April 1918. Ernest's parents (especially his father, who had hoped his son would also become a doctor) approved this "useful Christian service" and gave their blessing to his plans.

THE "FIRST" AMERICAN CASUALTY

On June 7, 1918, his first day at his new post in Milan, Italy, a munitions factory exploded and Hemingway was one of those dispatched to help. The factory was surrounded by bodies and splattered with bits and pieces of people, including fragments of flesh caught by its heavy barbed wire fencing. Fourteen years later his memories of the scene would form the basis of the section in *Death in the Afternoon* called "A Natural History of the Dead."

As fighting shifted to the south, Hemingway volunteered to man a relief station behind the lines at Fossalta di Piave; his duties would include bringing chocolate and cigarettes to the Italian soldiers at the front. In the middle of the night on July 8, Hemingway was delivering supplies near the front lines when he was hit by shrapnel from a trench mortar shell. He was seriously wounded in the head and both legs—although not as seriously (in number or severity of wounds) as his later war-tale exaggerations would have it. Early biographers took those claims as fact, along with tales of a heroic attempt to save an Italian soldier who had been mortally wounded by the same shell. Most later biographers (who had access to more records) believe that the fictional account of Lieutenant Henry's wounding in *A Farewell to Arms* comes closer to the truth of Hemingway's experience. In the book Lieutenant Rinaldi says, "They want to get you the medaglia d'argento. . . . Did you do any heroic act? . . . Didn't you carry anybody on your back?" And Henry responds, "I didn't carry anyone. I couldn't move."

However, as Kenneth Lynn observes, "when it came to handing out medals to their allies, . . . Italy's military commanders were proverbially generous." Hemingway—like Henry—was awarded the Italian Silver Medal.

Celebrated as the first American casualty of the war (although a fellow ambulance driver had been killed by Austrian fire a few weeks earlier), Hemingway and his wounds received a great deal of attention from the press. His sister Marcelline was watching a newsreel in a Chicago movie theater when he suddenly appeared onscreen, shown in a wheelchair at a Milan hospital.

Hemingway had been transferred from a field hospital to that hospital in Milan just four days before his nineteenth birthday. With eighteen nurses for a half-dozen wounded soldiers, patients received plenty of attention. One of his nurses, twenty-six-year-old Agnes von Kurowsky, a librarian from Washington, D.C., became his first serious crush. (At least one biographer noted similarities between Agnes and Hemingway's mother. Kenneth Lynn writes, "At five feet eight inches tall, Agnes was the same height as Grace and her chestnut hair was almost exactly the same color.")

After several months of recuperation and with the war over (as of November 11), Hemingway returned to the United States to a hero's welcome. He had proposed to Agnes and she had hinted that her answer might be yes. He planned to get a job and establish a home for them, and he was crushed and angered when he received a letter from her saying she had found someone else. Some of the anger shows in the tenth sketch in his second book, *in our time*, published in Paris: A nurse named Ag, who meets the wounded-soldier hero in a hospital in Milan and agrees to marry him, throws him over after he returns to the United States, writing him that "theirs had been only a boy and girl affair." (Hemingway also included a longer version of the vignette, titled "A Very Short Story," in his first book published in the United States, *In Our Time*. He changed the nurse's name and the locations for the second and later editions of the American version.) A more complex reworking of fact into fiction is found in the relationship between Frederick Henry and Catherine Barkley in *A Farewell to Arms*, in which the relationship holds firm but the heroine dies.

Back at home with his parents, Ernest initially took to his bed with a fever on receiving Ms. von Kurowsky's rejection. But he was soon working hard at writing short stories. Since these were invariably rejected by the magazines he sent them to, his mother became increasingly frustrated with him: he would not go to college, would not get a job, and would not even clean up his messy room. On his part, Ernest was furious that after all he had experienced and suffered, his mother still treated him as a boy. His mother's failure to treat him with what he felt was the proper respect was in vivid contrast to his treatment by the other residents of Oak Park, who often invited him to civic gatherings to speak about his experiences in the war and celebrated him as their own war hero.

Ernest accompanied his family to Michigan that summer, but he stayed mostly with friends. His mother complained that he was seldom around to do chores for her. When the family returned to Oak Park in the fall, he stayed in Michigan, renting a room in a boardinghouse in Petoskey and trying to make a living as a freelance fiction writer. In December he was invited to give his popular war-experiences lecture for the benefit of the Petoskey Ladies Aid Society. His dramatic tale impressed the audience, whose members included Harriet Connable, wife of the head of the F.W. Woolworth chain in Canada. The Connables offered Hemingway a job as companion to their son at their home in Toronto while they spent a winter vacation in Florida. To sweeten the deal, Ralph Connable promised to introduce the young writer to his friends at the *Toronto Star Weekly.* He accepted. His first article for the newspaper was published on February 14, 1920, and fifteen more articles followed in the next three or four months. At the Connables' insistence, he stayed on with them when the rest of the family returned from their vacation, but by late spring he was ready to return to Michigan.

Ernest was looking forward to a summer of fishing and loafing; his parents expected him to make himself useful around the summerhouse. By July his parents had become increasingly concerned. Not only had he refused to cooperate in their plans for him, he had become belligerent. Clarence, who was in Oak Park for most of the summer, had sent him five dollars to do some spraying; he kept the money but did not do the chore. On July 21, 1920, Ernest was twenty-one years old. Shortly after his birthday dinner at Windemere, his parents told him to stay away from the family home until he was invited.

Adding to the crisis was a secret midnight outing that two of Ernest's sisters and some of their friends decided to have on the night of July 26. The Hemingway girls, Ursula and Sunny, had persuaded Ernest and his friend Brummy (Ted Brumback) to come along as chaperones. When the empty beds were discovered, the two men were blamed. The affair was an innocent one, but the involvement of their neighbors made the situation worse: Mrs. Loomis, mother of two of the truant children, announced that "she would pack up and take her whole family back to Oak Park unless we could do something to get rid of those grown men loafing around." When Grace confronted her son, she told Clarence,

> Of course Ernest called me every name he could think of, and said everything vile about me. . . . Oh! But he is a cruel son. . . . [He] said "all I read is moron literature,". . . and asked me if I read the *Atlantic Monthly* just so someone would see me doing it. . . . He is distinctly a menace to youth.

Clarence was also sorrowed and outraged by his son. He wrote Grace, "He must get busy and make his own way, and suffering alone will be the means of softening his Iron Heart of selfishness."

For his part, Ernest portrayed himself as very put-upon and misjudged, claiming that he had done the work of a "hired man" that summer. He deeply resented both his parents' expectations and their treatment of him. But, as James Mellow notes, "Clarence and Grace had stuck to their principles, as they had been brought up to do in a world of values that were fading. And Hemingway, unable to forgive his father for being the man he was, reserved his scorn for his mother, whom he blamed for all the trouble."

ON HIS OWN

Hemingway decided to move to Chicago. There, in October 1920, he met Elizabeth Hadley Richardson. He later claimed to his brother, Leicester, that as soon as Hadley entered the room, "an intense feeling came over me. I knew she was the girl I was going to marry." And so he did, on September 3, 1921.

After a honeymoon at Windemere (he had achieved a wary reconciliation with his parents), the newlyweds were off to France. Hemingway was to be the *Toronto Daily Star*'s foreign correspondent in Europe.

Ernest had met Sherwood Anderson, a popular novelist, at the Chicago Men's Club. Anderson, recently back from France, had provided the Hemingways with letters of introduction to several important people there, including writers Gertrude Stein and Ezra Pound, and Lewis Galantière, an

American translator and writer who was well versed in French culture.

Galantière promptly invited the new arrivals to have dinner with him and his girlfriend. At dinner Hemingway challenged the translator to come back to the hotel for a little sparring. Catching him when his guard was down, Hemingway delivered a blow to the face that broke Galantière's glasses. It made an awkward end to the evening. (Over the years Hemingway would similarly challenge many other men—critics, authors, drinking buddies, a suitor of one of his sisters—men usually smaller than him, and nearly always less experienced in boxing. It was a peculiar and unattractive form of bullying that was seldom the "sportsmanlike" encounter he claimed.)

Fortunately the introduction to Gertrude Stein went more smoothly. Stein invited Hadley and Ernest to join her and her companion, Alice B. Toklas, for tea, and after that first meeting Stein and Hemingway developed a warm friendship. It was Stein who supplied the term Hemingway made famous in *The Sun Also Rises*, "the Lost Generation." ("All of you young people who served in the war. You are a lost generation.")

Hemingway also hit it off with Ezra Pound. Pound asked to see some of Hemingway's work, and quickly pronounced his poems "swell" and sent them off to *The Dial* in New York. They were rejected, as was the story Pound had proposed to publish in *The Little Review*, but the fact that he had made the effort bolstered Hemingway's belief in his own writing.

FOREIGN CORRESPONDENT

The Hemingways met many other writers and artists in Paris, and Ernest was working on poems and short stories with great dedication. But he also had a job. Even though he complained, after only three months in Paris, that "this goddam newspaper stuff is gradually ruining me," it was his position as a correspondent for the *Toronto Star* that paid the bills.

Reporting for the *Star* sent him traveling around Europe. He covered the 1922 International Economic Conference in Genoa, Italy, where his economic analysis was spotty but his descriptions of personalities and the rise of Fascism vivid. He and Hadley vacationed in Germany; he wrote articles on German inflation and the hostility of Germans toward those who benefited from the devalued German mark, and on the riot of a German mob protesting the high cost of living. In September 1922 the *Star* sent him to cover the last stages of the Greco-Turkish war. He wrote of Constantinople in panic, of the evacuation of the Greek army, of a twenty-mile column of refugees in bullock-drawn carts and of a woman giving birth in one of them as her frightened daughter watched. Then—after a brief trip back to Paris and Hadley—he was off to Lausanne, Switzerland, to report on the conference that would try to settle the territorial disputes between the Greeks and Turks. Here, just months after having written glowingly of Mussolini's rise to power (he had interviewed the Fascist Italian leader in Milan), he reversed his opinion and wrote scathingly of a man he now considered a fraud.

BUMBY

An unexpected event was soon to change the Hemingways' life: Hadley became pregnant. The couple would return to Toronto for the baby's birth. Hemingway managed to fit in a trip to Spain before they left; he had picked up on Stein's enthusiasm for the bullfight as ritual and was eager to see the confrontation of matador and toro in person. His passion for the spectacle would be illustrated some nine years later, in *Death in the Afternoon*, as well as in short stories and articles.

Another project to be completed before he left: checking the proofs and cover design for his first book, *Three Stories and Ten Poems*, which Robert McAlmon was publishing in Paris. Hemingway was also writing and revising vignettes for his second book published in Paris, *in our time*. (One of the new pieces was on the fictionalized death of a matador he had just seen and admired in Pamplona.)

Toronto, after Paris, was boring. He was working for the *Daily Star*, being sent out on what Hadley called "absurd assignments," often until two in the morning, by a boss who did not like him. He was away on assignment in New York when Hadley went into labor; their son, John Hadley Nicanor Hemingway, was born on October 11, 1922. (The infant was quickly nicknamed Bumby. In later years, he would be known as Jack to those who watched his television show on fishing.) Among the Christmas gifts Grace Hemingway would send her new grandson: a short dress like the ones in which she had dressed his father.

Having been sent out of town by his hated boss when Hadley was about to deliver led to a blowup at the office, and Hemingway was soon working exclusively for the *Weekly Star*, back under his old, more agreeable boss, J. Herbert Cranston. The feature stories he was writing now gave him more time to promote his first two books, but he was still itchy to return to Europe. He quit his job, and by mid-January the young Hemingway family was headed back to France.

PARIS, AGAIN

When *in our time* was finally published, Edmund Wilson reviewed both of Hemingway's books in *The Dial.* Wilson wrote that Hemingway, Stein, and Sherwood Anderson now could be considered a school, distinguished by "a naiveté of language, often passing into the colloquialism of the character dealt with, which serves actually to convey profound emotions and complex states of minds. It is a distinctively American development in prose." Although Hemingway would later work to dissociate himself from Stein and Anderson, he was grateful for the warm review.

He was already working on another book, his first to be published in the United States. *In Our Time* would include fourteen stories, interwoven with vignettes (including those from the Paris book, *in our time*). Calling it a masterpiece, James Mellow writes:

> Through the character of Nick Adams, the hero of many (though not all) of the stories of *In Our Time*, Hemingway created a fictional persona for himself and for his time. He announced themes that would carry him through a lifetime of work: the disappointments of family life, the disaffections of early love, the celebration of country and male comradeship, a young man's initiation into the world of sex, the consequences of marriage. In the interchapters, Hemingway recreated the destructive violence of battle and the ritual violence of bullfighting intended to give the larger chronicle of his times—the world of war and politics, of crime and punishment—that were juxtaposed with the more personal circumstances of the stories.

Hemingway's friend Don Stewart had been trying to find an American publisher for *In Our Time*, and finally succeeded in getting Boni and Liveright to offer a contract, which included an option for his next two books. Sherwood Anderson, who had just switched publishers to B & L, wrote a blurb of unqualified praise for the cover of the book.

A CAREER LAUNCHED

In Our Time, Hemingway's American fiction debut, received some enthusiastic reviews. But Hemingway was not happy. Many reviewers compared his work with that of Stein and Anderson, and he did not like the comparison. In fact, the identification with Anderson (compounded by his friend's enthusiastic blurb on the book's cover) drove Hemingway to write *The Torrents of Spring*, a scathing parody of Anderson's novel *Dark Laughter*. Banging it out in ten days, he decided to use it for a dual purpose: not only would it emphasize the separation between them, he would use it to get out of his contract with Boni and Liveright so he could publish with Max Perkins, F. Scott Fitzgerald's editor at Scribner's. (In his opinion, B & L was not sufficiently enthusiastic about his work.) The ruse worked. B & L would not publish a work so mean-spirited and harmful to another of their own authors, and refused to exercise their option. Hemingway joyfully turned to Perkins.

The Torrents of Spring was Hemingway's first book for Scribner's. Several biographers have found in it more than a parody of Anderson. A tale of a triangle between a man and two women that ends with the man's feeling empty as he gets the "new" woman, it echoes what was going on in Hemingway's life while he was writing it. Pauline Pfeiffer, an editor at the Paris office of *Vogue*, had decided she wanted Hemingway for herself. After a protracted chase, she got him: Hemingway somewhat sadly asked Hadley for a divorce.

FAMILY REACTIONS

Hemingway had earlier had six copies of *in our time* sent to his parents; his father, disgusted by the subject matter, had returned them to the publisher. Now, with the breakup of his marriage to Hadley, hints of alcoholism, and the publication of *The Sun Also Rises*, family tensions again came into the open. His parents were glad to see him successful, they wrote, but surely he could use his God-given talent to a higher purpose. Grace considered it a doubtful honor to have written "one of the filthiest books of the year"—her opinion of *The Sun Also Rises*. Despite the very favorable tone of the major critical reviews, she encouraged him to mend his ways: "I love you dear, and still believe you will do something worthwhile to live after you."

Hemingway fired off an angry response, accusing his mother of hypocrisy. The book was no more offensive than "the real inner lives of some of our best Oak Park families," he said, in a veiled reference to his own family life. He later wrote his father:

> I *know* that I am not disgracing you in my writing but rather doing something that some day you will be proud of. . . . You

could if you wanted be proud of me sometimes. . . . You cannot
know how it makes me feel for Mother to be ashamed of what
I know as sure as you know that there is a God in heaven is
not to be ashamed of.

Yet just one month later *Men Without Women* would be published by Scribner's. As Kenneth Lynn notes, the last story in
the book, " 'Now I Lay Me,'. . . with its devastating portrait of
Grace, was bound to bring shame to her."

FAREWELL THE STARVING ARTIST

While his parents did not appreciate his work, publishers, critics, and the reading public did. When *The Sun Also Rises* came
out in October 1926, the first printing quickly sold out. And
then the second, and soon the third. *Scribner's Magazine* and
Atlantic Monthly now sent checks instead of rejection letters.
At the same time, Pauline's wealthy family helped the couple
pay their expenses—her uncle Gus Pfeiffer, for example, offered to pay the rent on a nice apartment in Paris for the two of
them, and other relatives sent thousand-dollar checks as wed-
ding gifts. With *Men Without Women* scheduled for the fall of
1927, Hemingway abandoned his pride in his scruffy appearance and treated himself to some fancy new clothes.

He could afford to indulge his tastes on a much more ex-
pensive scale now. When Pauline announced she was pregnant and did not want to have her baby in Europe, Hemingway began looking around for a new base of operations.

KEY WEST

In March 1928 Pauline and "Papa," as Hemingway now liked
to be called, moved to Key West, Florida, where he set to work
on *A Farewell to Arms.*

Hemingway discovered that his parents were vacationing
in Florida and invited them to join him and Pauline. Grace
was in robust health, but his father had deteriorated alarm-
ingly. Plagued by diabetes and angina attacks and distressed
by the failures of his land investments in Florida, he made a
shocking contrast to his vibrant, self-satisfied wife.

Pauline had decided to have her baby in Kansas City, so it
was there that Hemingway continued work on *A Farewell to
Arms.* On June 17, he wrote a friend that he knew how the
novel was going to end. Eerily, ten days later his second son,
Patrick, was delivered, after a long labor, by Caesarean section—an event similar to the end of the novel. But while Pauline
survived childbirth, the fictional Catherine Barkley did not.

On December 6, Hemingway picked up his five-year-old son, Bumby, at the New York dock for his annual visit and boarded a train for Key West. At Trenton, New Jersey, he was handed a telegram saying his father had died that morning. He sent his son on to Key West in care of a porter and headed for Oak Park, where he learned his father had committed suicide.

Clarence had awakened that day with a pain in his foot, and before long he had decided it would lead to gangrene and amputation. (As a physician, he knew this was a common complication of diabetes. Added to his other physical, mental, and financial woes, it must have seemed too much to bear.) He killed himself around noon. His thirteen-year-old son, Leicester, heard the shot and found the body. (Those sounds and sights haunted Leicester—Ernest's only brother—for the rest of his life. In 1982, told that he would have to have his legs amputated because of diabetes, he too shot himself.)

Shaken by his father's suicide, Hemingway returned to Key West to rework, over and over, the ending of *A Farewell to Arms*. When it was finally published in September 1929, sales were brisk, and continued so even after the collapse of the stock market and the resulting financial panic in October. The reviews were superlative; from the royalties for this book he set up a trust fund for his mother to supplement the allowance he had begun sending her.

The Hemingways had been renting places in Key West for a couple of years, but in 1931 they settled into their own home. Pauline had fallen in love with a house on Whitehead Street, and her uncle Gus had purchased it for her as a gift. There Hemingway worked on a few short stories and on his bullfighting book, *Death in the Afternoon*, with a trip to Spain that spring and summer to take in the bullfights and evaluate the new bullfighters. While he was there, he observed the political unrest in the country, which would soon lead to civil war.

On November 12, 1931, Gregory Hancock Hemingway, Ernest and Pauline's second son (his third; he kept hoping for a daughter) was born. Like Patrick's it was a difficult Caesarean birth, and Pauline's doctor warned her not to conceive again. In April 1932 Hemingway "fled from the sound of a squalling infant" (as biographer Lynn puts it), heading for Havana for two weeks. He stayed for two months, marlin fishing in the mornings and working on *Death* galley proofs and another Nick Adams short story in the afternoons.

In September 1932 *Death in the Afternoon* was published. Initial reviews were mixed but generally positive.

ROAMING THE WORLD

Although he professed himself happy in Key West, by 1933 Hemingway was planning to spend several months in Havana for fishing, followed by a trip to Spain and an African safari. (Uncle Gus had offered to finance the $25,000 cost of the safari.)

In Spain he found both the bullfights and the new republic disappointing (he predicted another revolution). From there he joined Pauline in Paris, where it seemed all the news of old friends was depressing and everyone talked calmly about "the next war." While he was in Paris, Max Perkins sent him the early reviews for his latest collection of stories, *Winner Take Nothing*; critics called the book his worst writing and suggested that he was losing his ability to write. He was also unhappy with Scribner's for not properly promoting *Death in the Afternoon.*

After these depressing sojourns, Africa was a treat. Hemingway had contracted to write a series of "letters" for a new magazine, *Esquire.* In his first missive from Africa he wrote, "Nothing that I have ever read or seen has given any idea of the beauty of the country or the still remaining quantity of game." He would address that deficiency with *Green Hills of Africa* (which he misleadingly called "absolutely true autobiography") and short stories, especially "The Snows of Kilimanjaro" and "The Short Happy Life of Francis Macomber."

On returning to New York, Hemingway decided to buy a sleek power boat, to be delivered to him in Florida. He named it the *Pilar*, after the code name Pauline had used during their affair while he was still married to Hadley. But Pauline was not often invited to join the excursions on her namesake.

Green Hills of Africa was published in October 1935. Since Uncle Gus had paid for the safari that provided the material for the book, Pauline was treated so well in the book that one reviewer commented on the "delicacy of his love for his wife." Other reviews were less approving. By December Hemingway had entered a deep depression.

SPANISH CIVIL WAR

When civil war broke out in Spain in the middle of 1936, Hemingway was eager to be on the scene. When the North American Newspaper Alliance (NANA), a news service, asked him if he'd like to become a war correspondent again, he jumped at the chance. He would visit the country four times, in the spring and fall of 1937 and of 1938.

His marriage was deteriorating, so he was happy to get away from Pauline when he went to Spain ... but he did not like to be alone. He found a solution in Martha (Marty) Gellhorn, a journalist and author whose works had been compared, not unfavorably, to his own. They first met in December 1936 in Sloppy Joe's Bar in Key West. They shared a suite in Madrid during his first trip there, in spring 1937, and with his help she became an excellent war correspondent. (Unfortunately, his own reportorial skills were less stellar; NANA eventually dropped him as a correspondent.) And just as *The Torrents of Spring*, written while he was poised between Hadley and Pauline, foretold an unhappy end to the choices he would make, *The Fifth Column*, which he was writing "between" Pauline and Marty, foretold another marital mistake. (The three-act play would be published in 1938 in *The Fifth Column and the First Forty-Nine Stories*.)

He found himself more productive in Havana than in Key West, so he was often in Cuba during the summer of 1939. Marty Gellhorn was there, too; Pauline had decided to spend the summer in Europe. Marty had found and renovated an old farmhouse, the Finca Vigía, and Hemingway had moved in with her. He had put aside his novel *For Whom the Bell Tolls* until he learned how the Spanish war would turn out; now he returned to it, trying feverishly to finish it before war broke out in Europe. Before it was published in October 1940, World War II was well under way. The book was a runaway best-seller, with nearly half a million copies sold during the first six months after publication.

MARRIAGE, AGAIN. AND AGAIN.

Hemingway's divorce from Pauline and his marriage to Marty took place two weeks apart, in November 1940. Their honeymoon was an Oriental tour covering the Sino-Japanese War, she writing for *Collier's*, he for a new liberal daily, *PM*. They parted in Rangoon; she continued the tour (Singapore, Dutch East Indies), while he was eager to return to Cuba.

Back in Cuba, he volunteered the guesthouse of the Finca Vigía as the headquarters of a counterintelligence unit he would set up ("the Crook Factory") and the thirty-eight-foot *Pilar*, armed with bazookas and grenades, as a one-ship antisub task force. A friend at the American embassy got the American ambassador, Spruille Braden, to consider the plans. At Braden's request, the Cuban government authorized both the Crook Factory and the sub hunting.

While Hemingway roamed the Caribbean looking for subs, Marty accepted hazardous assignments in England, North Africa, and Italy in 1943 and 1944. This was not Hemingway's idea of wifely duties, especially since she was being highly paid for her reporting (while he was not). He sent her angry cablegrams ("ARE YOU A WAR CORRESPONDENT OR WIFE IN MY BED"). As he later explained to his sister Carol, "What I wanted was [a] wife in bed at night not somewhere having even higher adventures at so many thousand bucks the adventure." For her part, Marty wanted him to clean up his act: cut down the drinking, stop telling tall tales about the Crook Factory—and clean up his living quarters. But the writing was the main point of contention; Gregory Hemingway would remember his father's yelling at Marty, "I'll show you, you conceited bitch. They'll be reading my stuff long after the worms have finished with you."

True to form, he had another wife lined up before dispensing with the current one. He met Mary Welsh (Monks), a *Time* feature writer, in London, and quickly told her that he wanted to marry her. When she objected that they were both married to others, he allowed that the war might keep them apart for a while, but "just please remember I want to marry you."

Although journalists were not allowed to land with the troops, on D day, June 6, 1944, he was on a landing craft watching troops go ashore in France. Marty, however, had stowed away on a Red Cross hospital ship, and although she was not there on D day, she did "hit the beaches" on June 7, helping to evacuate the wounded. Hemingway never forgave her for her one-upsmanship. "Going to get me somebody who wants to stick around with me and let me be the writer of the family," he wrote to his son Patrick. By March of 1945 he and Marty had agreed to divorce. He divorced her in Cuba in December 1945; he and Mary, who had divorced her husband, Noel Monks, were married the following March.

BACK TO NOVELS

Hemingway found it hard to begin writing again after the war. His next novel, *Across the River and into the Trees*, could have used Max Perkins's guiding hands (Perkins died in 1947); the critics lambasted it. He returned to one of the books he had set aside when he had written *Across the River*. *The Old Man and the Sea*, published in 1952, was a phenomenal success. *Life* magazine published the entire text, with an

Albert Eisenstadt photograph of Hemingway on the cover, and sold 5,300,000 copies in two days. Even the critics proclaimed it a masterpiece. On May 4, 1953, he learned that it had been awarded the Pulitzer prize. The movie rights had been sold, and Spencer Tracy was to play the old man. Hemingway was back on top.

Look magazine offered to finance an African safari plus pay $10,000 for a 3,500-word story on the trip. Hemingway accepted, making another trip to Pamplona and a tour through Spain on his way to Africa. Once he was in Africa, this second safari became an adventure of an unintended kind: He and Mary survived not one but two plane crashes in two days. They arrived back in "civilization" (a town with medical facilities) to discover that their deaths had already been reported internationally.

When, in October 1954, Hemingway was told he had won the Nobel prize, he was ecstatic. But he wondered if his premature obituaries might have had as much to do with the award as *The Old Man and the Sea.*

DECLINE

Revolution was brewing in Cuba; having seen it coming in Spain, Hemingway recognized the ominous signs. After some of President Batista's soldiers shot one of his dogs, he and Mary decided to return to the States for the fall and winter of 1958–59. He was there, in Idaho, when he heard that Fidel Castro had taken Havana. He pronounced himself "delighted," then modified it to "hopeful." But it still seemed a good time to buy a house in Idaho, and a good time to plan a trip to Spain for the following summer.

In Spain that summer of 1959, the year he turned sixty, he was greeted wherever he went as a celebrity. But he was drinking heavily; that, with the irregular hours and travel tensions, led to kidney problems. His moods were capricious and sometimes irrational.

Having accepted an offer from *Life* for an article on bullfighting, he returned to the Finca Vigía to write it. By July 1960 he had reluctantly concluded he would have to go back to Spain to get photographs and check facts. Four days after his sixty-first birthday, the Hemingways left Cuba for New York and then Spain, expecting to return that fall. Before they could return, the farmhouse and its contents—including Hemingway's collection of works by artists Juan Gris, Paul Klee, Georges Braque, and others, and several thousand books—had been appropriated by the Castro government.

Meanwhile, in Spain during August and September, Hemingway was suffering a breakdown. (Mary had stayed in New York.) Paranoid and delusional, he mistrusted friends as well as strangers. His friends managed to get him on a plane to New York, where Mary hoped that he was just suffering from overwork and would recover with rest. But he did not. Difficult family relationships, a family history of depression and a lifetime of alcohol abuse, at least five concussions and many other serious injuries over the years, diabetes, high blood pressure (treated with reserpine, which can cause depression)—it is impossible to assign his mental and emotional problems to any single cause, especially since he refused to consider any "talking" psychiatric therapy. By the end of the year, doctors at the Mayo Clinic had begun administering a series of electroshock therapy treatments. (Developed in Italy in 1938, the therapy, also known as electroconvulsive therapy, or ECT, had been found to help reduce the symptoms of patients suffering from major depression and delusional depression. There were also reports that it could cause memory deficits, which doctors believed were limited and temporary.)

The therapy seemed to help for a time, but his paranoia gradually returned. Worse, he was convinced that the shock treatments had destroyed his ability to write. Attempts at suicide were followed by more therapy, but there came a night when it all fell apart. He crept downstairs, retrieved from its locked cabinet a favorite shotgun, loaded it, and killed himself.

CODA

In a November 1962 *Esquire* article called "The Big Bite," Norman Mailer examined the troubling question of how Hemingway could have committed suicide, which seemed the antithesis of all he believed in. He concluded:

> It is not likely that Hemingway was a brave man who sought danger for the sake of the sensations it provided him. What is more likely the truth of his own odyssey is that he struggled with his cowardice and against a secret lust to suicide all his life, that his inner landscape was a nightmare, and he spent his nights wrestling with the gods. It may even be that the final judgment on his work may come to the notion that what he failed to do was tragic, but what he accomplished was heroic, for it is possible that he carried a weight of anxiety with him which would have suffocated any man smaller than himself.

CHAPTER 1

Themes in *The Old Man and the Sea*

READINGS ON
THE OLD MAN AND THE SEA

The Old Man and the Sea as Fable

Delbert E. Wylder

In the following selection, Delbert E. Wylder argues
that *The Old Man and the Sea* is a fable that portrays the archetypal journey of the hero. Yet Hemingway hints that the old man's journey has not
been as meaningful as those of other classical heroes. The old man can only hope, at best, for a conditional victory—one that includes defeat. Wylder is
the author of *Hemingway's Heroes*, from which this
selection has been excerpted.

The last "novel" to be published during Hemingway's lifetime was *The Old Man and the Sea,* a work which Hemingway would identify as a new form. The precise generic clas-
sification is more or less inconsequential although it is
apparent that the work is a completely developed fable in the
form of a very short novel. The protagonist of the book
brings to full circle Hemingway's use of the mythic hero, for
Santiago is again a hero with a different face. He is a modern adaptation of what Joseph Campbell has called the
"saint or ascetic, the world-renouncer." The true world-renouncer, Campbell explains, follows a pattern

> of going to the father, but to the unmanifest rather than the
> manifest aspect: taking the step that the Bodhisattva re-
> nounced: that from which there is no return. Not the paradox
> of the dual perspective, but the ultimate claim of the unseen
> is here intended. The ego is burnt out. Like a dead leaf in a
> breeze, the body continues to move about the earth, but the
> soul has dissolved already in the ocean of bliss.

Like the Bodhisattva, Santiago too renounces the final step
and returns to the world. After having successfully battled
against the gods and won, the modern hero finds that he can
return only after a torturous and defeating experience that
strips him of everything except the symbol of his victory. . . .

[Critic] Earl Rovit has specifically identified the novel as the journey of the "quest" hero, but it is important that the journey does not follow the typical pattern of the archetypal hero in his quest.

In many respects the story calls forth the basic quest pattern, such as in the myth of Jason and the Golden Fleece. But instead of a young man, the hero is an old fisherman. After many trials the hero attains his reward, but is then beset with vicissitudes as he tries to bring the boon back to mankind. Jason, through the help of the gods, is able to return with the Golden Fleece. Santiago is able to return only with the skeleton of his success. The major differences, then, are the ages of the heroes and the final results of their expeditions. In a detailed examination of the story of Santiago it becomes evident that there are also a number of shifts of emphasis and a number of differences from the typical quest that become important. And what becomes obvious, I think, is that *The Old Man and the Sea* is essentially a story of defeat. As a fable, however, it also suggests the potential of man despite inevitable defeat. . . .

The journey is not just a realistic battle with a big fish nor one in which a man tests his integrity against great odds; it is a romantic attempt on the part of a champion to test the gods of the universe; perhaps it is even an attempt at regeneration. What it finally becomes, however, is a statement about the "burning out" of the ego in the godlike attempt and the ultimate defeat on the way back to the community of men.

The quality of fable is introduced early in the work, not only through the omniscient author's description of the old man, but in the description of the comparative serenity of the man's existence. Santiago is well-loved by almost all around him. He has been unlucky for almost three months, but his community still favors him. Although there are people who laugh at him, most of the fishermen are sad about his loss of luck, and the boy is thus able to provide him with food gathered from the community of friends. . . .

With the aid of the boy, Santiago is ready to go out to the sea on his archetypal quest. . . .

SANTIAGO AND NATURE

Within the sea are things that man both loves and hates. Santiago does not, as critics have suggested, love all things "both great and small," like the Ancient Mariner. He hates the poisonous and treacherous Portuguese men-of-war and loves the turtles for eating the dangerous creatures. There is thus a dualism of good and evil within the sea, just as the sea itself may give favors or do "wicked" things. The old man, with the patience of a Job, has usually accepted the fact that the sea can withhold its favors. He has had even longer runs of bad luck. But this time he purposely changes his patterns to change his luck. He isolates himself from the community of fishermen and journeys farther out than ever before.

As he travels out, a man-of-war bird appears. "The bird is a great help," the old man says, and he follows the course of the bird. The bird and a school of fish symbolically lead him over the edge of the world of men, across the threshold into the world of gods. After catching a tuna for bait, he continues until he hooks the marlin. He would like to avoid a battle, to have an easy victory, and he hopes that his catch will be easy to control.

But Santiago has been overanxious. The marlin has the hook in its mouth. When the hook sinks in, the marlin begins the long pull toward the northwest. The battle with the gods will not be an easy one. As the fish pulls, Santiago thinks of how the fish has chosen the direction because of Santiago's own treachery.

> His choice had been to stay in the deep dark water far out beyond all snares and traps and treacheries. My choice was to go there to find him beyond all people. Beyond all people in the world. Now we are joined together and have been since noon. And no one to help either one of us.

Santiago's choice was to extend himself beyond the human, and thus to extend human treachery out into the world of the gods. He has intentionally gone beyond the limits of mankind.

During the first night, another fish takes one of the baits, "a marlin or a broadbill or a shark," but Santiago cuts it loose. He deliberately chooses to follow the quest of the big fish rather than to sacrifice his opportunity for what might be an ordinary catch. . . .

Finally, the crucial moment arrives, and Santiago is ready to bring the fish in for the kill. He is tired, his hands are "mush" and his vision is blurred. He tries to bring the fish in close, but fails repeatedly. Each time he feels himself "going" but always he thinks he will "try it once again." Finally, he brings the fish close.

He took all his pain and what was left of his strength and his long gone pride and he put it against the fish's agony and the fish came over onto his side and swam gently on his side, his bill almost touching the planking of the skiff and started to pass the boat, long, deep, wide, silver and barred with purple and interminable in the water.

The old man dropped the line and put his foot on it and lifted the harpoon as high as he could and drove it down with all his strength, and more strength he had just summoned, into the fish's side just behind the great chest fin that rose high in the air to the altitude of the man's chest. He felt the iron go in and he leaned on it and drove it further and then pushed all his weight after it.

The fish makes its last surge and the sea is discolored with its blood. The old man, having called forth strength from beyond his physical nature, feels faint and sick.

The old man looked carefully in the glimpse of vision that he had. Then he took two turns of the harpoon line around the bitt in the bow and laid his head on his hands.

He has had a visionary glimpse, and for a moment he pauses to rest. Rovit suggests that "this angling vision into the heart of mysteries cannot be brought back to the community of men." This is true in terms of Hemingway's presentation, of course. There is a choice for Santiago to make, however, in terms of the heroic adventure. Joseph Campbell states that the human responsibility of the return has often been refused. Many heroes have taken up residence forever in the "blessed isle of the unaging Goddess of Immortal Being." But Santiago is not Melville's Ahab, motivated by a monomaniacal dream of vengeance. Santiago is a fisherman, and part of the reason for his quest has been to bring back food. His has been a purposeful quest in terms of his community. Santiago immediately recaptures his mortal senses. His sense of human duty and responsibility is too strong to allow him to regress into the bliss of the final cause. The work that he has generally thought of as a man's duty, however, he now thinks of as "slave work."

"Keep my head clear," he said against the wood of the bow. "I am a tired old man. But I have killed the fish which is my brother and now I must do the slave work.". . .

SANTIAGO'S DOUBTS OVER HIS ACTIONS

He keeps looking at the fish to make sure that the adventure in which he has been engaged has been a real one. The two

THE BEST FICTION HAS THE QUALITIES OF FABLE

The novel is nearly a fable. The best fiction, at its heart, always is, of course, but with his particular diction and syntax, Hemingway's stories approach fable more directly than most, and never so directly as here. It is the quality of his fiction at its very best, the marvelous simplicity of line. ('"Be calm and strong, old man", he said.') There has been another strain in his fiction, to be sure—his personal ambition to become a character in a tall tale, folklore as opposed to fable. That is the weaker man pushing aside the great novelist. The strain glimmers once in this story when we are told of the old man's feat of strength in his youth: 'They had gone one day and one night with their elbows on a chalk line on the table and their forearms straight up and their hands gripped tight.' Take it away.

The true quality of fable is first of all in the style, in the degree of abstraction, which is not only in some ways Biblical but is always tending toward the proverbial rhythm. ('The setting of the sun is a difficult time for fish.') Next, it is in the simplicity of the narrative, and in the beautiful proportion (about three-fourths to one-fourth) of its rise and fall. Finally, of course, it is in the moral significance of the narrative, this fine story of an ancient who goes too far out, 'beyond the boundaries of permitted aspiration.'

Mark Schorer, *New Republic*, October 6, 1952.

---

of them, like brothers, start the return journey. . . . They are hit by sharks. The first is a Mako shark with as much beauty and dignity as the marlin. It has no fear and makes a direct attack. Santiago kills this shark with the harpoon. He has already begun to wish that he had not killed the marlin. "It might as well have been a dream, he thought. I cannot keep him from hitting me but maybe I can get him." After the shark is dead Santiago begins to wish the killing of the fish had been a dream. Then he thinks,

> "But man is not made for defeat," he said. "A man can be destroyed but not defeated." I am sorry that I killed the fish, though, he thought.

He recognizes that there will be more sharks, and he has lost his harpoon in the big Mako. Between the time that he kills this shark and the attacks that come later, he has time to think about the morality of killing the great marlin. Twice he goes over essentially the same ground.

The pattern that leads him into thinking about sin begins with the return of hope.

> It is silly not to hope, he thought. Besides, I believe it is a sin. Do not think about sin, he thought. There are enough problems now without sin. Also I have no understanding of it.

But he continues to think about it. Then he thinks again about the killing of the fish, and once more he is conscious of sin.

> Perhaps it was a sin to kill the fish. I suppose it was even though I did it to keep me alive and feed many people. But then everything is a sin.

And after trying to quit thinking, he faces the question more honestly, admitting that he was motivated by pride.

> . . . and he kept on thinking about sin. You did not kill the fish only to keep alive and to sell for food, he thought. You killed him for pride and because you are a fisherman. You loved him when he was alive and you loved him after. If you love him, it is not a sin to kill him. Or is it more?

Santiago cannot resolve the question regarding sin, but he does learn the answer to his question about hope. As the great Mako shark comes in to destroy the fish, Santiago attacks. Hope is replaced by something else.

> The old man's head was clear and good now and he was full of resolution but he had little hope. . . .

The old man continues to fight the treacherous sharks, killing them, too, with malignancy. He maintains his resolution, but he is becoming even more sorry that he has gone beyond "human limits" to seek out this fish. The sharks' treachery makes him more aware of his own treachery. He addresses the fish. He says aloud, "I wish it were a dream and that I had never hooked him. I'm sorry about it, fish. It makes everything wrong." He continues, "I shouldn't have gone out so far, fish, . . ." "Neither for you nor for me. I'm sorry, fish." Throughout the day he battles the sharks. By dusk the marlin is half gone. Santiago is getting closer to land. His proximity to the shore and safety makes him think quite differently about the human society that he had so willingly left behind him at the beginning of his quest.

> I cannot be too far out now, he thought. I hope no one has been too worried. There is only the boy to worry, of course. But I am sure he would have confidence. Many of the other fishermen will worry. Many others too, he thought. I live in a good town.

The emotional pull now is toward the community of men. He begins to feel alone, and to miss the boy. Then something with regard to the fish comes into his head, and he apologizes.

> "Half fish," he said. "Fish that you were. I am sorry that I went too far out. I ruined us both. But we have killed many sharks, you and I, and ruined many others."...

THE HERO'S RETURN

Santiago's battle with the sharks on the return journey may be divided into three phases. First is his initial encounter with the Mako shark that makes a direct attack. Second is his gradually losing battle with the *galanos* during the day. In these battles, he loses all of the pointed weapons that are capable of killing the enemy. At the beginning of the return journey, he has hope for a successful return until he sights the first shark. This is replaced by resolution, although he knows that he will never get the marlin back to the land. As the third and final stage of the battle begins he has lost all hope for a successful return with his prize. As the darkness descends, he begins to hope again. This time, however, he does not hope for success; he hopes only that he will not have to fight again. But the gods do not give him any luck, and the sharks attack. There is nothing he can do but club the fish as they tear at the marlin's body. He fights until he uses up all weapons and there is no meat left on the carcass. He has continued to fight with resolution, even after he feels something break within him. His philosophy that man was not created for defeat is shattered. "He knew he was beaten now finally and without remedy," and he pays no attention to the sharks picking the bones of the carcass. As Lewis notes, "He must be completely humiliated before he can emerge from the sea as the new man."

The battle has been lost, and his reaction insignificant. There is no bitterness. He still believes that the forces of nature, the wind and the sea, may be his friends as well as his enemies. He recognizes how easy his progress is now that the battle is over and he has been beaten, and he is very much aware of what has defeated him. His answer to his own question about what has beaten him is "Nothing. I went out too far." He has been beaten by his own treachery.

When he finally arrives at the harbor, he carries the mast back up the hill to his house and falls into bed. No one is there to help him beach the boat, and he carries the cross-like mast up the hill in silence and without thinking. He falls once, watches a cat that is going about its business at night with no knowledge of man's tragic struggles, and then goes on. He must sit down to rest five times on his way. Only at the beginning of this climb does he turn to look at the skeleton. Joseph Campbell says that "the modern hero" must find his own way.

> It is not society that is to guide and save the creative hero, but precisely the reverse. And so every one of us shares the supreme ordeal—carries the cross of the redeemer—not in the bright moments of his tribe's great victories, but in the silence of his personal despair.

Santiago has carried his cross up the hill in the silence of his own despair. The skeleton of the fish, spiritual symbol of his victory, will be misunderstood by most of the world. The actual evidence of his battle and of the return is what affects the boy. Manolin, having already seen the skeleton of the fish, sees Santiago's hands and begins to cry. When he leaves to get coffee for the old man, he passes the fishermen who are measuring the skeleton. He does not express interest in their findings; he merely indicates his belief that it was an eighteen-foot fish. He does not care that they see him crying, and his only concern is that they do not disturb Santiago. Again, when he is complimented on his own catch as he orders the coffee, he begins to cry. The old man is asleep when Manolin returns with the coffee, and the boy waits patiently. In the first words Santiago speaks, he admits his defeat.

> "Don't sit up," the boy said. "Drink this." He poured some of the coffee in a glass.
> The old man took it and drank it.
> "They beat me, Manolin," he said. "They truly beat me."

There is ambiguity as well as a deliberate protective duplicity in Santiago's confession. Physically, the sharks beat him, but he explains it as though he is telling about the sharks as hostile and powerful forces beneath the sea. The indefinite "they" emphasizes the symbolic aspect of the treachery within the sea on the way home. Manolin makes a clear distinction.

> "*He* didn't beat you. Not the fish."
> "No. Truly. It was afterwards."

Santiago makes it clear that he was not defeated in his quest against the gods. He informs the boy that it was only after his victory that he was defeated by the treacherous forces in the dualistic sea. But he does not mention the truth that he had found for himself—that he had gone out too far. He does not mention his own human treachery to the boy, although he hints at it when he tells Manolin that he is no longer lucky. . . .

A Symbol of Victory

Santiago must at least unconsciously recognize the importance of the quest. Although he is willing to admit to Manolin that he has been defeated by the sharks, he gives the boy directions for equipping the boat for another trip in which Manolin is obviously going to lead. He does not, as he well might, warn the boy that he was beaten, as he has admitted to himself, because he went out too far. As in his refusal to warn the little bird flying to shore, he recognizes that Manolin too will have to find out for himself, will have to take his chance "like any man or bird or fish."

The fishermen who see the marlin's skeleton see in it only the representation of the biggest fish that has ever been caught in their knowledge. The tourists in the concluding ironic passage are unable even to recognize the type of fish, and in a sense confuse the very nature of good and evil and man's relation to it. With perhaps even greater irony, in the final paragraph of the novel, the old man lies in his bed dreaming of the young lion cubs playing on the beach. Santiago is the hero who has been out to touch the great secrets. He has killed the big fish and has felt its heart with his harpoon. But he has also learned that he can bring nothing home from the battle with the gods except a symbol of his victory, and that in the bringing home lies the great defeat. . . .

Loss

Santiago's motivations have been saintly, but sinfully human as well. The result of his ordeal has been the recreation of his own heroic ego in Manolin. He has achieved this victory through suffering. What he has achieved for himself is also significant. Santiago is too complex to appear as the typically pure fabular hero. He has restored his own ego through the quest and its influence; though he has conducted himself as a saint, his motivations have been those of human pride.

Though the boon that Santiago has brought home has been only a symbolic one which is misinterpreted by almost all who see it, he has learned much from his journey. He has lost the pride that has given him a feeling of superiority. He has learned to miss his fellow men, and it is not incidental that, just before Manolin leaves, Santiago cautions the boy not to forget to give the head to Pedrico. . . .

Once again the concept of loss is evident, and the quest is suggested as a meaningless and self-destructive venture. Most important, the suggestion that there are no pure heroes emphasizes the irony of the baseball conversations early in the novel. It is not through the inspirational victories of the Joe DiMaggios that the true heroism is displayed and that the "heroic" character of mankind can be formed; it is through the recognition of man's ultimate defeat, which he endures with resolution and courage and which brings him into an acceptance of reality, that a conditional victory is won.

The Old Man and the Sea Is an Allegory of the Artist

Wirt Williams

After publishing his first novel, *The Enemy*, Wirt Williams earned his Ph.D. in English and American literature at the University of Iowa. A professor of English at California State University at Los Angeles, Williams is the author of six novels. In this selection, taken from his critical work *The Tragic Art of Ernest Hemingway*, Williams points out that *The Old Man and the Sea* can be viewed as an allegory of the artist and his creation: The fish is the work of art and Santiago's struggle with it is the agony of the artist attempting to achieve the masterpiece.

Immediately on publication, it was perceived that *The Old Man and the Sea* was layered with meanings beside the naturalistic, which was itself an overpowering universal. In attendant reviews and essays in books, Baker, Breit, Schorer, and Young considered all of the cardinal interpretations.[1] These were the naturalistic tragedy, the Christian tragedy, the parable of art and artist, and even the autobiographical mode. Baker saw the realistic and Christian tragedies as almost inseparable and the dominating aspect of the book; he pointed also to the art-artist and autobiographical strands. Young felt that the triumph of the work was the triumph of classical tragedy and saw it as the ultimate fusing of Hemingway's personality and art; he too saw the art-artist implication and the autobiographical elements as closely linked

---

1. Carlos Baker, "The Marvel Who Must Die" and "The Ancient Mariner," in Carlos Baker, *Ernest Hemingway: The Writer as Artist* (Princeton: Princeton University Press, 1972), 288–328; Harvey Breit, review of *The Old Man and the Sea*, in *Nation*, CLXXV (September 6, 1952), 194; Mark Schorer, "With Grace Under Pressure," *New Republic*, October 26, 1952, p. 20; Philip Young, *Ernest Hemingway: A Reconsideration* (State College: Pennsylvania State University Press), 1966, 121–33.

and noted the Christian symbology. Breit was most impressed with the universality of the realistic tragedy, and Schorer with the work as a drama of the artistic struggle, a struggle by no means confined to the author.

Most subsequent criticism, and it has been voluminous, has proceeded essentially from those lines set down so immediately. However, the possibility that the novel is a deliberately constructed, three-tiered (and possibly four-tiered) fable perhaps should be considered. The view here is that the naturalistic, the Christian, and the art-artist modes are all constructed carefully enough to stand alone, yet are so tightly laminated that no joining shows, and that the autobiographical is intuitive. Together these are, in final aspect, an unbroken unity. And the commitment to fable that Hemingway exhibited in *Across the River and Into the Trees* is consequently even more in evidence here. . . .

The art-artist fable . . . declares itself by the cumulative force of its connotations. And like both the naturalistic and Christian modes, it functions as tragedy by itself, though naturally all are stronger perceived as one unified tragic work than as an addition of separates.

Seen as such a separate, the art-artist drama, however, is simple and direct. The fisherman is the artist, fishing is art, and the fish the art object. Santiago the archetypal fisherman becomes Santiago the archetypal artist. Even more uniquely, this fish is the great work of art, and Santiago's struggle with it is the agony of the artist attempting to achieve the masterpiece. Forces destructive of art inevitably mutilate the masterpiece and block the artist from deserved recognition. But he has already won his triumph of the self over this material catastrophe in the performance of the great artistic act, and he reinforces it in his achievement of serenity in his abiding creative vision. The act is indestructible, and transcendence is built into it.

Simultaneous with this generic mythos is an autobiographical one, which makes Santiago a projection of Hemingway himself. It is only half-developed, sometimes almost ostentatiously visible, finally almost submerged in the larger design. That it may be intuitive and unplanned simply makes it more intriguing. In this, Santiago is Hemingway, once the greatest of all in his métier but now fallen and derided; Hemingway of scrupulous craft *and* burning personal vision; Hemingway, who has not been destroyed by his economic activity—journalism—but has used it both to survive and to nourish his real work; Hemingway, who will come back from scorn and again defeat all others with a master achievement; Hemingway, who considers he has done it and sees his just prize wrested from him by a hostile reviewing establishment; Hemingway, who is still the tragic hero, serene in the knowledge of his feat and comforted by his vision. So Santiago is thus Hemingway as artist—and champion—as well as the universal artist.

This pattern is absorbed by the larger generic pattern, however, and that larger one makes certain fairly distinct assertions about the process of art and working at art. These may be conveniently, if a little Teutonically, seen as grouping into a few cardinal categories.

FISHING ALONE

Imperative and isolation. Both of these are first sounded in the very first line—Santiago fishes, and he fishes alone—though their import begins to emerge forcefully only when the voyage begins. At sea, he reflects repeatedly that he was "born" to be a fisherman and that he must think of no other purpose; when the fish is towing him far out to sea, he reflects that he has no help in the challenge of the masterpiece except what comes from himself, and the surrounding sea reminds him of his aloneness. He asserts that he will prove his commitment to his work again though he has proved it many times before, and he reiterates his determination to follow the imperative—execute the masterpiece, kill the fish—until death. His affirmation is stronger after he has glimpsed the awesome shape of the masterwork.

Nor does his fidelity ebb after he has executed the great work—tied the fish alongside; it is simply directed against new challenges. He must try to protect the work against those forces that would destroy it, and possibly all art, and he reiterates that hopeless determination as he battles the sharks. These represent not only reviewers and critics here but imperception, exploitation, that whole part of the apparatus of cynicism that attaches itself to each of the arts and will destroy it if unchecked.

And the artist strong enough to obey the imperative will be strong enough to perceive an alleviation of the aloneness, though it will not be provided by other men until the task is over. It appears, rather, in an awareness of the unity of the cosmos and all living things in it, which comes gradually to the striver in the depths of his self-imposed exile for his art. Santiago acknowledges as he sees a flight of ducks against the sky that he knows "no man . . . [is] ever alone on the sea"; later, the physical part of his masterpiece destroyed in total catastrophe, he can embrace the very element which, in the largest sense, destroyed it: the sea itself. He affirms himself at one with the sea, the wind, the town where he lives, the destroyed masterpiece itself. And though he grieves for this ruined master work, he appears to have attained the deep, ultimate happiness of the noblest tragic hero, in his role as artist as well as in his other identities. He knows both that the great creation will always be his, and that he himself is as ultimately responsible for its destruction as he was for its execution.

Craft, method, and luck. The first two are constantly in view in Santiago's careful preparation before he goes out—his systematic check of his gear and provisions, the care he gives to the smallest tasks, from stowing his gear to baiting the hooks—and is crystallized by his careful maintenance of his lines at exact depths and positions. He keeps them more precisely than anyone else, he reflects—not impossibly the author's tribute to the author as craftsman. He has not had luck, but he prefers skill to luck.

Yet from the first Santiago acknowledges the supreme importance of that other element, luck. He is "unlucky," the boy is on a "lucky" boat, eighty-five may be a "lucky" number. Is luck the same as that psychic indefinable, inspiration? It would seem not. Santiago speaks later of having violated his luck when he went "outside too far." Yet the shark is carefully presented as an inevitability, not an accident, and the catastrophe as a pure cause-and-effect event. Perhaps he means his *hubris* destroyed the luck that would have protected him from the harshnesses of order. For luck seems to lie outside the orderly world, to be almost a caprice of the cosmos in action, as Tyche, the goddess of luck, was considered to be essentially unrelated to any other force, even the Fates, a force apart from everything, by those Greeks of the first century B.C.

Yet luck has some kind of relationship with inspiration, the text suggests. It is luck that may reward skill, in the example of the carefully maintained lines, and luck may manifest itself in inspiration, or idea, donnée, subject.

THE HARD LABOR OF LUCK

It may manifest itself there, or anywhere, but it is not the same thing. Inspiration, imagination, creativity—whatever it is named—is one of the two prime and almost equal partners in the hard labor of art. Imagination and discipline-craft are fixed as such partners in the image of the two hands and the fish they work together to bring in (Baker's Trinity image). Santiago proclaims all three brothers: masterpiece, craft, and imagination. But which hand is which? That ancient maxim, "the left hand is the dreamer," suggests the left as the delicate and unpredictable, even uncontrollable component of imagination, with the stronger and ever faithful right as discipline and skill. Santiago's denunciation of the left as "traitor" reinforces that view, and it is the right hand with which he wins the hand wrestling championship. The left might even be characterized as the unconscious and the right as the conscious.

The powerful black man Santiago beats in the "championship" wrestling contest with his right hand seems pretty obviously the devil in the Christian tragedy, but what is he here? Less clear: perhaps the despair and doubt of both self and the validity of art that assails every artist from time to time, perhaps autobiographically one writer whom Hemingway felt he had to beat and did beat to become "champion." Who? The guess here is Faulkner, but it may be a bad guess; the whole concept has to be avowed as tenuous, and all nominations consequently speculative.

The mysterious and the miraculous. There is something in the making of the superwork that lies beyond that partnership of craft and inspiration, however, and even beyond the capricious and not at all holy element of luck. This is the awesome benediction of mystery and miracle; the artist's own exertions, however wise and strenuous, can only take him so far. Then the great work is *bestowed* or it is not.

The first intimation of mystery impending appears, dim and precise yet with unmistakable connotation, as Santiago starts out in his skiff. The silence of the sea, broken only by the sound of unseen oars stroking, is an evocative context for Santiago's reflection that he is going "far out"; in addition to its hubristic declaration, it suggests the start of a voyage into the unknown, into mystery. These notes intensify, first subtly, and then directly and powerfully when the fish takes the bait.

Santiago's prayer-like invocations more directly belong to the Christian story but also strongly point to the emerging aspect of the miraculous in art. The fish is "unbelievably heavy," "of great weight," and Santiago marvels at his size as he envisions him "moving away in the darkness." The mystery of the bestowed masterpiece is constantly deepened. When Santiago is actually taken in tow by the fish, the work assumes control of its creator; for four hours he does not see it, and he thinks of the fish as "wonderful and strange," of a great and mysterious age. He reflects that the fish chose to stay in "deep dark water" and that he found him "beyond all men"; their joining is thus hinted as a kind of miracle as well as mystery, in the art parable as in the others. These aspects are constantly strengthened by his reflections on the size and nobility of the marlin and flower in the great death leap, the Ascension image in the Christian mode. The "great strangeness" he feels in remembering it and the dimmed eyesight that accompanied it, make that sight a different kind of holy vision for the artist: this is the grail of the achieved masterpiece he has always sought. It may be glimpsed and briefly possessed if it has been truly earned, but it is not permanent and it cannot be shared—not even by fellow artists who can at least understand its magnitude and the agony it represents.

The emerging oneness of artist and masterpiece. Even greater than the agony of execution is the agony of the destruction of the achieved masterpiece, for by this time, creator and work have become one. They have been "brothers" during their battle; when the fish is tied to the boat, they almost immediately become a single entity. Which is bringing the other in, he wonders; when the sharks mutilate the fish, he feels as though their teeth are ripping him. Later he tells his sorrow to the fish; by going too far out—creating too big a work—he has destroyed them both. This may be the climax of the development of their ever-tightening oneness. The thematic implication is instantly perceived: in the execution of the masterpiece, the masterpiece ultimately becomes part of the artist. What is inflicted upon it is inflicted upon him. Here, Backman says, Hemingway's fusion of active and passive, slayer and slain, finds its strongest expression.

FATE OF THE MASTERPIECE

The masterpiece is always maimed by the events that are subsequent to its creation: that is, it can never be completely and truly perceived by any but the artist. It never survives intact in the dignity and honor it deserves. Developed directly by the battle and its outcome, this theme is culminated by the last image of the fish: a skeleton with a tail and fin that is now floating garbage, awaiting total oblivion by the tide.

But though the masterpiece itself may be destroyed (by hostility, misunderstanding, and misrepresentation, maiming critical attacks), the achieving of it cannot be. The execution of the work of art is not only a performance but a fact: though it may not survive in space, it will survive in time and in the greatest dimension, memory. This is one of the implications of the awe of the other fishermen at the size of the fish's skeleton and their understanding of Santiago's ordeal which attended its taking.

Another is that the achievement of the work of art is understood by the elect, the brothers in the art, and it exists as example and inspiration to them. Concomitantly, the non-elect, those who do not know, in their obtuseness confuse the achievement of the work with the destruction of it: the destroyers are honored, the creator shunned. This last, bitter irony is rendered in the comment of the tourist gazing at the ruined fish: "I didn't know sharks had such handsome beautifully formed tails."

But for the true artist, for him who has reached awareness in his suffering and achieving, all of this recedes into unimportance. For him, only one thing endures and is of final significance. This is his vision, from which this work and all the artist's work comes, and it is projected in the last line, "The old man was dreaming about the lions."

The fate of the work, as caught in the destruction of the fish by the sharks, is one of those phases of action that inevitably seems to belong in the autobiographical parable, too. An early view had it that the fish was this very book and the sharks were the critics, an inaccurate precognition since they had not had a chance at it during its composition and liked it when they did. The better surmise probably is that they suggest the undervaluation that Hemingway felt reviewers had accorded him. . . .

The artistic vision. The lions that are decisive symbols in the other modes of the story are equally strong as a synthesizing and culminating image in the tragedy of art. The dream of lions is a great sustaining force for the old man as he lives in failure and charitable scorn; he summons them in his most agonized hours during his ordeal of execution, and at the end they supply the final definition to this layer of tragedy as to the others. His great work as a physical entity has been destroyed. His achievement has not only been ignored and unperceived by those who do not know, but these give credit for achievement to the very ones who have destroyed it: the tourists think the remains of the fish are those of a shark, and comment on the shark's beauty. But Santiago does not care: he has achieved the sublime indifference of the artist to everything but his deepest vision of beauty and life and of his work in relation to them. It is unshakable and enduring and will always renew him. He is dreaming about the lions: he is warming himself with the artistic vision. One would judge that this is Hemingway's idealized self-portrait in the crucial dimension— not himself as he knew he was, but himself as he knew he ought to be, the artist as he ought to be.

CRITICS, CRITICISM, AND THE ARTIST

The sharks are forces of destruction in every fable of the book but they are splendidly unlimited in each. Yet, as with the lions and the other images in the complex symbology, their unclosed, larger identities also enclose quite exact lesser identities. Thus at the first level they are all the unnameable elements of a hostile universe that crush man, but they are more narrowly nemesis; in the Christian tragedy, they are all the forces against Christ, but touches link them uniquely with the Pharisees; here, they are the huge conglomerate of the forces that assault all art: exploitation, neglect, public indifference and ignorance, self-doubt, despair—and of course the reviewers and critics. That much advertised last identity is not "wrong," but it is only one part. Still, it is the most interesting part, apparently to the author and literate public as well. And certain aspects of the author's attitude toward the sharks as reviewers-critics have not been so widely observed as his hostility.

The hostility, in fact, is directed, and carefully directed, toward only the "scavenger" sharks—the reviewers who are frantic to play follow the leader. The first shark, the Mako, is accorded a scrupulous if unloving accolade: he is as beautiful as the marlin except for his jaws, he fears nothing, he is built "to feed on all the fish in the sea." This authentic, super critic is the equal of the artist but is different in function, a differentiation that is underscored by the resemblance of his teeth to "cramped" human fingers (the cramping suggesting a freezing of the creative function). Exercising his admittedly "noble" purpose, he attacks bravely. But Santiago has only contempt for those scavengers who can only follow their better and bite the fish "where he had already been bitten." Thus, the great critic is as great as the great artist—but those who can only follow him and each other are cowards and unworthy.

Sharks more diffusely suggest the entire critical activity: when they are dismembered, stripped, and processed, as critics break down a creative work, at the "shark factory," they make a stink that permeates the bay. Yet Santiago makes a bow to the critical activity when he acknowledges taking shark liver oil regularly; it helps the eyes, as a little pure criticism helps the artist's vision.

The economic, physical sustenance of the artist. This is the most quotidian of all the considerations developed here and it becomes most interesting when the author uses it in a candid autobiographical representation of the relationship between journalism and literature. Yet careful justice is done to the more general parallel: the old man is artist, as he was Christ at the Last Supper, when the boy brings him the gift of food to strengthen him for the next day's fishing. For after his long bad luck Santiago cannot buy for himself, and without physical nourishment, the spiritual labor of art cannot be performed. The repeated rituals of eating smaller fish in the boat, more important as communion ceremonies in the Christian fable, here stress the need of continuing physical and economic sustenance for the artist in his most elevated creative endeavor. They may be more interesting, however, as a suggestion that the artist proceeds from his own lesser work to the greater, gaining strength through the smaller for the creation of the larger. And among Santiago's reflections on the fish are many with a definite economic facing. He wonders if taking the fish were a sin, though it will keep him alive and "feed many people." He thinks of the money the fish will bring in the market, enough to feed him through the winter. And he declares that he did not kill the fish just to stay alive himself—his imperative to create and pride in work were infinitely stronger than economic necessity.

Yet the biggest image of the economic activity—as the sharks were of the reviewers and critics—is the turtles, and within this generic representation there is a more piquant one of Hemingway himself. More generally, turtles and any-thing pertaining to them are objectifications of the economic process—the turtles themselves, their eggs, "turtling," and turtle boats. Broadly speaking, the artist must resort to some activity or practice to support himself—hiring out on turtle boats that catch them or eating their eggs. Sometimes this lower activity not only keeps the artist alive but instructs and tempers him for his real work: the practice of art—catching big fish. But the turtles are both larger and infinitely more provocative when seen as objectifications of journalism and even of journalists in Hemingway's own career. When the boy tells Santiago that Santiago's years on the turtle boats did not hurt his eyes, Hemingway is declaring that his stretches of journalism did not hurt his own artistic vision. When San-tiago speaks of eating turtle eggs to keep himself strong in the winter, the author is not only speaking of the physical nourishment but of the experience that can be fashioned into art which journalism has given him; the figure recalls certain lines from the introduction to his collected short sto-ries, "In going where you have to go, and doing what you have to do, and seeing what you have to see, you . . . blunt the instrument you write with." But the instrument can always be rewhetted, he contends. When Santiago says he feels no mysticism about turtles, Hemingway is saying he feels none about the newspaper or magazine business, as many former newsmen profess to do. He expresses friendly contempt for the ordinary journalists, the "stupid loggerheads," but admi-ration for the excellent journalists—*i.e.,* his good friends in the ranks—by praising green turtles and hawkbills for their "elegance and speed and great value."

So the book demonstrates overwhelmingly the author's turn toward fable that became markedly evident in *Across the River and Into the Trees.* And these layers of the story are constructed to the measure of many kinds of tragedy, that fuse as the levels of the work fuse. Whether one considers this novel to be Hemingway's best or not depends on what he expects from a novel. But none is more powerful as an ex-pression of the tragic, and none should define him so finally as one of fiction's most powerful, and subtle, prophets of the tragic vision.

Aging in *The Old Man and the Sea*

Stanley Cooperman

Stanley Cooperman, formerly a professor of English at Simon Fraser University in Vancouver, British Columbia, is a writer of poetry, fiction, and literary criticism. In the following selection, Cooperman focuses on what he claims was a difficult subject for the perennially virile Hemingway—old age. Cooperman contends that even in this novel, the old man is unrealistically virile, accomplishing a task that would be impossible for a man his age. Cooperman concludes that Hemingway, both in fiction and in life, was unable to accept the inevitable aging process.

The virtues of the Hemingway hero had always been the virtues of the young: to kill "cleanly" and risk being killed; to drink manfully, speak simply, love beautifully (and briefly), and to avoid all entanglements of either responsibility or complexity. As critic Harry Levin remarks: "The world that remains most alive to Hemingway is that stretch between puberty and maturity which is . . . a world of mixed apprehension and bravado before the rite of passage, the baptism of fire, the introduction to sex.". . .

So essential is the "proper" confrontation of death to the work of Ernest Hemingway, that the problem of growing old seems quite irrelevant; few of his heroes are likely to grow old, and none of them will live to die in bed if they can possibly help it. As to a man outliving the days of his sexuality: this is simply too horrible to contemplate. Even the hunter in *The Snows of Kilimanjaro* dies of a wound rather than of old age, and at the time of his death, furthermore, is served by a sophisticated woman—a tribute to his strength and at least one kind of potency.

For Ernest Hemingway, far more than for most men, the

spectre of age was a terrible spectre indeed; the very virtues upon which he had based his art and his life were virtues of the young. Even in his later years Hemingway was delightfully "boyish" (or regrettably so, depending on one's point of view); the problem of age was never far from his mind nor, for that matter, from his conversation—and in this connection Lillian Ross's *New Yorker* piece on Hemingway (May 31, 1950) is of particular interest. "As you get older," said Hemingway, "it is harder to have heroes, but it is sort of necessary."

The problem, of course, is to decide what sort of heroism is possible as a man gets older, and in this respect Hemingway in 1950 was still looking backward rather than forward, so that for him (as for Robert Cantwell in *Across the River and Into the Trees*) old age itself was simply a matter of holding on to youthful appetites and youthful abilities as long as one could. "What I want to be when I am old is a wise old man who won't bore," he remarked to Miss Ross, while Mrs. Hemingway was saying "Papa, please get glasses fixed," and while the waiter was pouring wine:

> "I'd like to see all the new fighters, horses, ballets, bike riders, dames, bullfighters, painters, airplanes, sons of bitches, cafe characters, big international whores, restaurants, years of wine, newsreels, and never have to write a line about it. . . . Would like to make good love until I was eighty-five. And what I would like to be is not Bernie Baruch. I wouldn't sit on park benches, although I might go around the park once in a while to feed the pigeons, and also I wouldn't have any long beard, so there could be an old man who didn't look like Shaw." He stopped and ran the back of his hand along his beard, and looked around the room reflectively. "Have never met Mr. Shaw," he said. "Never been to Niagara Falls either. Anyway, I would take up harness racing. You aren't near the top at that until you're over seventy-five. Then I would get me a good young ball club, maybe, like Mr. Mack. . . . And when that's over, I'll make the prettiest corpse since Pretty Boy Floyd. Only suckers worry about saving their souls. Who the hell should care about saving his soul when it's a man's duty to lose it intelligently, the way you would sell a position you were defending, if you could not hold it, as expensively as possible, trying to make it the most expensive position that was ever sold. It isn't hard to die." He opened his mouth and laughed, at first soundlessly and then loudly. "No more worries," he said. He picked up a piece of asparagus and looked at it without enthusiasm. "It takes a pretty good man to make any sense when he's dying," he said.

The note of buoyancy combined with uncertainty, of readiness for death juxtaposed with fear of aging, of awareness of the inevitable combined with an almost wistful assertion of youthful power, and—finally—a kind of subdued self-perspective in which Hemingway seems to be doubting his own verbal posture—all these clashing elements were intrinsic to Hemingway's own position, as they were to the position of his protagonist in *Across the River and Into the Trees.*

A FEAR OF PASSIVITY

From the jumble of hopes for continued youth and fears of age, however, one element emerges as perhaps the greatest fear of all—a fear that had been close to Hemingway from the crisis of his World War I experience: that is, the fear of passivity, the nightmare, a recurrent nightmare for Ernest Hemingway, in which the individual is deprived of his manhood by becoming an object rather than originator of action. Whether sitting on a park bench and "waiting for death," or growing crochety and senile in an easy-chair, or whining and complaining in a hospital bed (while the hands of stranger-women clean the body and obscenely kill the soul), the over-riding fear is not loss of life ("It isn't hard to die," said Hemingway) but loss of will: the failure of manhood itself. And it was the divinity of manhood—a *mystique* defined by the sacred trinity of willed sacrifice, pride, and endurance—which Hemingway worshipped (and worried) throughout his life.

The problem, in short, was not how to avoid becoming an old man, but rather how to avoid becoming an old woman—and whether indeed an individual could be one without becoming the other. Whether Hemingway himself ever achieved a satisfactory solution to this dilemma is not for us to judge, although the circumstances of his death would indicate that he could not and would not abide a final weakening of those powers which were so intrinsic to the protagonists of his stories. . . .

If the early Hemingway had been an almost legendary figure of youthful and virile adventure, the older Hemingway would take up the role of Grand Old Man, the battle-scarred veteran, the aging but still indomitable combatant. Hemingway "The Champ," indeed, would become "Papa" Hemingway—the Citizen of the World still rough-edged and manfully poetic, but mellowed by experience and years, and come to full bloom as a connoisseur of life, bullfighters, women, fishing, and war.

The resources of age rather than the powers of youth

would henceforth be Hemingway's public role, and this was to provide the substance for his literary role as well. For *The Old Man and the Sea*, published in 1952, is the story not of youthful disillusion, or youthful political idealism in a framework of social affirmation, or youthful love in a world of chaos, or youthful frustration and anguish (bolstered by a code of manly non-sentiment), or not-so-youthful reminiscence relating to youth itself, but rather the story of an aged champion for whom power of will has replaced the power of flesh, and the wisdom of true pride and humility has replaced the arrogance of either simple pessimism or romantic self-sacrifice.

Humility and true pride, however, are not qualities likely to be possessed by the Crusading Idealist (such as Robert Jordan in *For Whom the Bell Tolls*), or by heroes of nostalgia (such as Colonel Cantwell in *Across the River and Into the Trees*), or by protagonists of alienation—protagonists who, like Frederick Henry in *A Farewell to Arms*, refuse to play the game of life (and death) if the rules are not of their liking. The qualities of humility and pride must be forged in the smithy of a man's own soul; only when the individual neither requires nor uses external crutches—either of affirmation, negation, or nostalgia—can he achieve that power of selfhood (which for Hemingway is synonymous with manhood) that old Santiago the fisherman achieves in his open boat, alone with his pain, his endurance, his love for the noble marlin that is his opponent, his defeat, and his ultimate triumph.

To Live

This triumph, of course, is a victory in spiritual terms—for it is only in spiritual terms that a victory can ever be real. Ultimately, the only "Cause" is a man's own being, his own truth; romantic love is an illusion of youth, and political or social motivation is either so complex as to be meaningless, or so corrupt as to defeat its own rhetorical purpose. Unlike Robert Jordan, Santiago does not attempt to justify his struggle in terms of externals; unlike Frederick Henry, he does not attempt to worship a sacred object—a kind of "Love-Goddess" for whose sake all things may be sacrificed. For Santiago, the only justification for life is living, and the only justification for death is dying: he is a fisherman and the marlin is a fish, and—joined together by a larger pattern in which each is merely a part—they fulfill their true roles.

The relationship between Santiago and the marlin is self-contained and self-meaning; not only is their struggle without hate, but—because the struggle itself is a link in that holy chain of life-and-death whose sole reason is its own existence—the contest becomes an act of love, almost of worship. And for Ernest Hemingway (much to the irritation of his more socially oriented or religiously orthodox critics) no act of worship could be defined in terms of group therapy. Santiago is indeed timeless; an aged monument to that power of will which finally emerges as the only means to defeat age itself, he remains a monument that stands for and by nothing but its own existence. His sainthood consists not in redeeming temporality, but rather in willing its irrelevancy.

The Old Man and the Sea, in short, marks a return on Hemingway's part from some attempt at social involvement to justify action, to an examination of action itself—and a hymn of praise to the sacred nature of such action, when purified by will and uncorrupted by external cause. "From the first eight words of *The Old Man and the Sea*," says Robert P. Weeks ("He was an old man who fished alone . . ."), "we are squarely confronted with a world in which man's isolation is his most insistent truth."

ACTION AS TRUTH

Human isolation: the basic *fact* of our existence, the "insistent truth" that men so often disguise by verbiage or theories, by titles or property, by all the various cosmetics and comforts offered by society, by entrenched religion, or by fleshly lusts called (or miscalled) spiritual allegiance, that they forget the isolation itself. Only in Santiago's old age, when the lusts of the flesh have cooled and the egoism and ambition of youth are no more than distant echoes, does he *act* in such a way that the act becomes its own truth: that is, he achieves divinity of manhood by means of the ritual or trinity of action consisting of willed sacrifice, pride, and endurance.

That such a ritual of manhood has only a limited relationship to brotherhood or unity in the orthodox sense, is indicated by the fact that Santiago himself despises and hates those forms of life which are neither worthily beautiful nor noble; if he kills but loves the great marlin, he butchers and spits at the scavenger-sharks, and his attitude toward the

Portuguese man-of-war (the bladder of "beautiful poison" that floats by his boat) is one of unrelieved loathing.

There is nothing of "love thine enemy" in Santiago's attitude toward those forms of life which either through appetite or a passive show of poison (or, as in the case of the tourists at the end of the book, simple ignorance) are outside the pattern of nobility and beauty, forms of life which—because they risk nothing, do not fight purely, or feed on carrion—provide no means for a man to celebrate the sacred ritual of his own manhood.

This theme of the "initiated" versus the "outsider" is, of course, a recurrent one throughout Hemingway's work, which celebrates a brotherhood of the *worthy* and noble rather than any sort of universal love. The very definition of worthiness and nobility, moreover, depends upon whether the creature in question (bull, fish, or woman) is capable of being used, or *absorbed*, into the ritual of manhood. Since this ritual is a means (indeed, for Hemingway the only means) of establishing non-temporality through assertion of will, "nobility" becomes a matter of usefulness, while "beauty"—always in terms of the ritual itself—is defined according to its manageability.

The story of Santiago, then, clearly represents a return, or rather, a re-emphasis and intensification, of the theme of isolation—the individual confronting his own destiny, and redeeming this destiny by means of a ritual of manhood which becomes its own justification. Having survived the great strength of his youth, Santiago has passed beyond all merely material ambitions and desires. There is a transcendent glow about the old man, who is himself a symbol of noble creation—that is, willed creation—with its sorrow and glory, pain and love. Divinity itself, after all, is Supreme Will ("Let there be light!" says the voice of God) rather than desire; as the embodiment of ageless will, Santiago the fisherman (who dreams of "lions") becomes an echo of the divine.

An Allegorical Old Age

Part of the dramatic effect of *The Old Man and the Sea*, however, may be weakened by the fact that Santiago—despite his use of wisdom instead of mere strength, and of knowledge and wit instead of mere arrogance—is in many ways a romantic picture of old age itself. His very old-ness is monumental and rock-like; his endurance becomes a statement of desire rather than a human reality. For Ernest Hemingway, looking toward his own old age and attempting to construct a means of coping with it, the vision of Santiago must indeed have seemed a noble possibility. That the Santiago-solution is largely allegorical, however, is something that Hemingway could not or would not face: it is not, after all, every old age that can go out to sea in an open boat and catch giant marlin.

In the refusal (or inability) of Ernest Hemingway to see old age in any other terms but the values of pride, sacrifice, and endurance—the ritual of will he worshipped all his life (in Santiago's case forged and made harder rather than softer by old age itself), and in his insistence that the old man must be a young man grown tougher and purer, Hemingway may well have been setting up his own final tragedy.

The Old Man and the Sea Is a Love Story

Linda W. Wagner

In the following selection, Linda W. Wagner traces the theme of love throughout *The Old Man and the Sea*. Wagner contends that the book's central theme is love between the old man and Manolin, and concludes that their relationship is perhaps the most realistically drawn of all Hemingway's characters. Wagner has published critical essays in a variety of periodicals, including *Swanee Review, Satire Newsletter*, and *Paris Review*. She is the author of books on William Carlos Williams and Denis Levertov and a professor of English at Michigan State University.

After *The Old Man and the Sea*, Hemingway tended to be more at peace; in fact he wrote in August of 1952 about the Santiago story, "It's as though I had gotten finally what I had been working for all my life." The focus in this essay, then, is on Hemingway's last great satisfaction, the lyric novel that may be his greatest because in it all segments of the book— structure, imagery, word choice, characters, plot—create a single organic whole. Hemingway began as a poet and so he ended—and, well aware of Dylan Thomas' remark that the greatest poems have in them both love and death, he captured in *The Old Man and the Sea* several great loves, and a truly noble death. . . .

T.S. Eliot may have been thinking of Hemingway's writing as well as Djuna Barnes's when he commented in his introduction to *Nightwood*, "it is so good a novel that only sensibilities trained on poetry can wholly appreciate it. A prose that is altogether alive demands something of the reader that the ordinary novel-reader is not prepared to give." With Hemingway's fiction (as with the Imagist poems that preceded it by a decade) each word counts. . . .

Excerpted from Linda W. Wagner's "The Poem of Santiago and Mandolin," in *Modern Fiction Studies*, vol. 10, no. 4, Winter 1973–74, pp. 518–529. Copyright © 1973 by The Johns Hopkins University Press. Reprinted by permission of The Johns Hopkins University Press.

By focusing on the immediate action, Hemingway follows Imagist doctrine and also avoids the sentiment inherent in his choice of hero. Santiago is pure pathos—alone except for an unrelated boy, poor, comfortless, unlucky, and old; yet because Hemingway presents him as proud and courageous, aligned with the arch young lions, that is the way we see him. . . .

Perhaps this is one of the most difficult of the Imagist tenets to employ, the fact that the author controls without interfering. He presents, he renders the story; but his control is limited to the selection of details. . . .

THE DETAILS

Hemingway's choice of the singular noun *shirt* in his brief opening description of Santiago is one such essential detail:

> Once there had been a tinted photograph of his wife on the wall but he had taken it down because it made him too lonely to see it and it was on the shelf in the corner under his clean shirt.

The reader is led quickly through the impressions—a photo, and colored at that, must have been a great tribute to his love; then Hemingway recreates his sadness, in removing the photo; then he reinforces Santiago's poverty: *the* shelf may well have been the only shelf, just as the single shirt was his only change. In one sentence Hemingway has conveyed both Santiago's passion and his poverty. . . .

As his experiments with language in his earlier novels had shown, Hemingway was also concerned with this rhythmic identity as an integral part of the whole effect. The rhythm of *The Sun Also Rises* is laconic, abrupt; of *For Whom the Bell Tolls*, moderately smooth, with much longer sentences. Hemingway's attempts to use the Spanish language, and the more personal pronoun forms, were ways of attaining the flavor—at least partially a rhythmic concern—of the Spanish people (the duration of the word *thee* is longer than *you* no matter how slowly the latter is said). . . . But nowhere does Hemingway match so well the language of his persona with the narrative voice of the novel. Santiago's tranquillity sets the pace for *The Old Man and the Sea*, in keeping with his slow, chary, and deceptively uncomplicated speech.

The passage describing Santiago's baits also illustrates the somewhat idiosyncratic use Hemingway makes here of the compound structure, particularly the connective *and*. In its simplest position, the *and* coupling suggests that there is no judgmental relationship between the clauses connected: "He was an old man who fished alone in a skiff in the Gulf Stream and he had gone eighty-four days now without taking a fish." It is not *because* he fishes alone that Santiago has caught nothing. The simple statement of apparent fact does what it purports to do, puts down the facts, with no causation or blame.

Hemingway achieves the same kind of objective tone when he uses the structure in more emotional situations, "The old man had taught the boy to fish and the boy loved him." Perhaps Manolin did love Santiago partly because of his having taught him, but rather than oversimplify the relationship, Hemingway again uses the simple coupling which leaves more to the reader's own insight. The structure—for all its apparent simplicity—is thus suggestive. . . .

DIALOGUE

It is one matter to look at single words and sentences and nod sagely, thinking, "Yes, that's Hemingway's 'one clear sentence,' and there is the 'no ornament except good ornament'"; it is more impressive to see all these single elements joined into a longer passage which works, and conveys surprising richness. The page of dialogue between Santiago and Manolin essentially presents their past relationship, their present love for each other—and the effect that love has on Santiago—all amid more commonplace detail about the village and the fishing process.

"How old was I when you first took me in a boat?"

"Five and you nearly were killed when I brought the fish in too green and he nearly tore the boat to pieces. Can you remember?"

"I can remember the tail slapping and banging and the thwart breaking and the noise of the clubbing. I can remember you throwing me into the bow where the wet coiled lines were and feeling the whole boat shiver and the noise of you clubbing him like chopping a tree down and the sweet blood smell all over me."

"Can you really remember that or did I just tell it to you?"

"I remember everything from when we first went together."

The old man looked at him with his sun-burned, confident loving eyes.

"If you were my boy I'd take you out and gamble," he said. "But you are your father's and your mother's and you are in a lucky boat."

"May I get the sardines? I know where I can get four baits too."

"I have mine left from today. I put them in salt in the box."

"Let me get four fresh ones."

"One," the old man said. His hope and his confidence had never gone. But now they were freshening as when the breeze rises.

In Manolin's comparatively long memory of the fish, Hemingway writes his usual active prose, relying on the many *-ing* words, but he more importantly resolves the boy's memories happily. Even though Santiago is "clubbing" the fish, his action seems as natural to the boy as "chopping a tree down," and the heavy blood smell he recalls as "sweet." That a five-year-old child had such a reaction to what must have been a gory and frightening scene shows clearly the trust he had in Santiago. Hemingway gives us further proof of the old man as trust-inspiring in his description of his "sun-burned, confident loving eyes," and then goes on to show in turn the power of Manolin's love on him, with the closing image. By placing the descriptions of Santiago throughout the section, Hemingway keeps the old man before us, even when Manolin carries most of the dialogue. And by establishing tone through nature images, he reinforces the impression of Santiago as sea-like, old, strange, proud, and unbeaten.

The relationship between Manolin and Santiago is poignantly done, particularly when one considers that the boy appears in only one-fifth of the novel—in the first eighteen pages and the last six. The structure of the book is thus like that of *The Sun Also Rises*, with Jake and Brett together in Parts I and III, as are Manolin and Santiago. Yet when Santiago is alone, he thinks often of the boy, and his thoughts of him become a kind of refrain.

It begins, "I wish I had the boy," and then modulates into "If the boy were here" finally reaching its climax in a threefold repetition, as the coils of line tear Santiago's hands,

If the boy was here he would wet the coils of line, he thought. If the boy were here. If the boy were here.

Santiago has no time to pray, he tells God in his humorous attempt to bargain, but his thoughts of Manolin come at points of crisis and—structurally—seem to substitute for the prayers another man might be saying. That this effect is intentional—Manolin as Santiago's only hope, only love—is restated later when Santiago justifies killing the marlin,

Besides, he thought, everything kills everything else in some way. Fishing kills me exactly as it keeps me alive. The boy keeps me alive, he thought. I must not deceive myself too much.

Using structure as well as immediate presentation, Hemingway drew this all-encompassing love relationship, perhaps the most convincing of those in any of his novels. When Manolin says, "I remember everything from when we first went together," we accept his exaggeration, as Santiago does, as evidence of his selfless love for the old man. His willingness to bargain, to beg, to steal for food and supplies for him—and to go against his parents' wishes—is further evidence of that generous relationship. . . .

MANOLIN AND THE OLD MAN

Manolin wants everything good for Santiago; there is no jealousy between competing fishing boats here. He is confident in his position with the old man; there is no timidity or artifice. One of the best evidences of the latter is the fantasy Santiago and the boy create about the yellow rice and fish. Only very confident lovers joke (as Santiago does with God). Such scenes create the aura of tranquillity, of surety, that this novel maintains throughout. Like Shakespeare in *The Tempest*, Hemingway has realized the value of humor in the midst of the life-and-death struggle that the book really is, and he uses it well: the old man's thoughts about Joe DiMaggio's bone spur, and his childlike wondering about it, occur at some of the highest peaks of action. And the comic dialogue between Santiago and Manolin about fear is a skillful touch of the raspberries to any former Hemingway reader. To come from Robert Jordan's near-obsession with fear, fear as an index of manliness, to Santiago's mocking comments on the baseball teams is progression indeed:

"The Yankees cannot lose."
    "But I fear the Indians of Cleveland."
    "Have faith in the Yankees my son. Think of the great DiMaggio."
    "I fear both the Tigers of Detroit and the Indians of Cleveland."
    "Be careful or you will fear even the Reds of Cincinnati and the White Sox of Chicago."

Santiago—and Manolin in his tutelage—seems to be almost beyond man's usual concerns with mortality—hence, his "strangeness" and perhaps his complete resolution. . . . Yet Hemingway includes enough detail to show that Santiago is a realist, not a romantic; he knows he will have to use "tricks" on the fish because his strength is not what it was when he was young. And he accepts his fate realistically, too, knowing that he "went out too far." The fish—though an impossibility—was not impossible to catch; it was only bringing it back such a long distance, unscathed, that was impossible. . . .

HEMINGWAY'S NARRATIVE SKILL

By the time of *The Old Man and the Sea*, Hemingway had learned not only to move easily between first person and omniscient (and here to include dialogue for more necessary insights); he had also learned to give the reader didactic help at crucial moments. Rather than have us believe what Santiago says—that the pain is nearly comfortable—Hemingway tells us how it really was. And rather than have us slide over the moon-sun passage, he adds a summary im-

---

A BOY'S MATURATION
Robert Donald Spector highlights the old man's role in guiding Manolin into manhood.

No interpretation of Ernest Hemingway's *The Old Man and the Sea* can afford to ignore the significance of the change in Manolin, the boy, in the course of the story's development. For much as "The Killers" is concerned with Nick Adams's growing up, the new Hemingway tale describes the process of a boy's maturation.

The old man provides an object lesson for the boy. His experience is living proof that greatness cannot be defeated, that it is deserving of faith, and that it achieves its own destiny regardless of fortune. The boy moves out from under his parents' domination—as he distinguishes luck from skill.

When the old man's forlorn sail looks "like the flag of permanent defeat," the boy is forced to abandon him by his father's decree. "It was papa made me leave. I am a boy and I must obey him," he tells the old man. Papa, he says, "hasn't much faith." Papa, who has no understanding of greatness—even greatness of baseball managers, had told the boy "that the old man was now definitely and finally *salao* . . . the worst form of unlucky."

It is the old man who understands greatness and reprimands the boy's lack of faith—even in the baseball Yankees:

"The Yankees cannot lose."

"But I fear the Indians of Cleveland."

"Have faith in the Yankees my son. Think of the great DiMaggio."

age a few pages earlier, so that Santiago's position is crystal-lized in our minds. It is all hopeless.

> The old man had seen many great fish. He had seen many that weighed more than a thousand pounds and he had caught two of that size in his life, but never alone. Now alone, and out of sight of land, he was fast to the biggest fish that he had ever seen and bigger than he had ever heard of, and his left hand was still as tight as the gripped claws of an eagle.

Soon after this, we have one of the few flashbacks in the book, as Santiago thinks of his Indian wrestling with the strongest man on the docks. They had gone one night and one day, and, for no rational reason, Santiago had won. So Hemingway tells us, in effect, that spirit can go a long way. It cannot, however, overcome everything. . . .

By shifting emphasis from catching the fish to staying with it, Hemingway changes the nature of the story. In the

> "I fear both the Tigers of Detroit and the Indians of Cleve-land."
> "Be careful or you will fear even the Reds of Cincinnati and the White Sox of Chicago."

But the old man knows that the boy is not lacking in faith. He has always provided the boy with an example, and the boy has acknowledged to him, "There are many good fishermen and some great ones. But there is only you." But this now is the supreme test, the important example:

> "I told the boy I was a strange old man," he said. "Now is when I must prove it."

In the last he is successful, and the success helps the boy take the important step to manhood. He knows that the man has not been beaten—at any rate, not by the fish. He knows that luck is not the answer and that when a boy sees the truth he must act beyond his parents' wishes:

> "Now we fish together again."
> "No. I am not lucky. I am not lucky anymore."
> "The hell with luck," the boy said. "I'll bring the luck with me."
> "What will your family say?"
> "I do not care . . ."

Obviously, Manolin, whom the old man had jestingly called a man at the beginning of the story, is no longer a boy.

Robert Donald Spector, *Explicator*, March 1953.

course of *The Old Man and the Sea*, he shows repeatedly Santiago's doing what he as man "had to do," and much more, until he finally waits, unarmed, for the last sharks, wondering "what can a man do against them in the dark without a weapon?"

It has been called existential, the fact that Hemingway gives his hero this dilemma, and makes him face it. But how similar the whole situation is to that of the scene in Faulkner's *The Unvanquished* when Bayard Sartoris asks, "How can you fight in the mountains, Father?" and the answer comes, "You can't. You just have to." *The Old Man and the Sea* is the novel Faulkner admired. For it is the first one Hemingway had written in the thirty years in which the hero stood it all. And lived.

The catharsis here, in this spent resolution of Santiago's struggle, must remind any reader of the effects of Greek tragedy. The classic intensity of focus is evident in the limitation to three characters, the nearly single setting (village, ocean, village), the three-day time span (unified by the single action), and the resolution of that single action. So tightly unified is the story, in fact, that some of the telescoping of time is so heightened that it creates irony. As Santiago pulls on the line, for example, Hemingway writes,

> This will kill him, the old man thought. He can't do this forever. But four hours later the fish was still swimming steadily out to sea.

The juxtaposition of time information with Santiago's incorrect "knowledge" does more than convey fact; it also foreshadows the falsity of many of Santiago's expectations. And we are reminded again of the Hemingway thesis: even the greatest of men can seldom be in complete control of all circumstances.

Structurally, too, Hemingway emphasizes this axiom. It takes Santiago ninety-four pages to get the fish and only eighteen to lose it to the various sharks. The concentration, even in terms of space and detail, falls on Santiago's purely voluntary exposure to danger. . . .

MANOLIN'S REACTION

Santiago's duty is only to himself and his ideals; similarly, only those who know him well, who understand him, can judge him. Therefore, Hemingway concludes the novel by letting Manolin give his reaction to Santiago's experience, fittingly, in actions as well as in words: crying, warming and rewarming Santiago's coffee, and keeping guard as the old man sleeps. Here, love is a secure and confident relationship.

The actual ending of *The Old Man and the Sea* works perfectly to complement the rest of the book. It is no deliberate Christian ploy to have Santiago carry the mast up the hill and then lie face down on his bed (this is the falling action of an exhausted man, not a person going to bed). For those who read these last ten pages as evidence of Hemingway's Christ symbolism, one must suggest that Santiago's not saying the promised prayers provides an antidote to that interpretation. Instead, we must view the last few passages as (1) summation of the theme that runs, obviously and yet skillfully, throughout the book—man's incredible ability to survive, and more, to dare; to make it, whole in the spirit and body; (2) a return to the enduring love that Manolin gave and Santiago lived for; (3) a necessary ending to the apparent "plot"—Santiago alive, his reputation vindicated, and the marlin skeleton disposed of; and (4) one of the most masterful of Hemingway's exercises in juxtaposition.

Once Santiago is asleep, focus shifts again to Manolin whose tears of joy and sorrow, occurring three distinct times, are the best single testimony to Santiago's courage. Then the last few pages of the novel shift setting kaleidoscopically: Manolin watching Santiago, going for coffee, talking with the crowd gathered near the skeleton, talking with Santiago, and then returning to the village. As the boy hurries back and forth, we sense the reactions of the entire village and even of the outsiders—those uninitiated observers who usually appear in a Hemingway novel, but often to the detriment of any total effect. Here, however, after the laconic dialogue of Manolin and Santiago, with even his evident suffering described only as "Plenty," the ending image of the tourists' ignorance has a triple-edged effect. The evidence of Santiago's greatest catch is now garbage and, as such, has no meaning for any but the initiated. Even when the waiter tries to explain what has happened ("Tiburon." "Eshark."), the tourists hear him incorrectly. In the vapid "I didn't know sharks had such handsome, beautifully formed tails," Hemingway has caught the tone of facile indifference he despised. Yet in this novel—rather than belabor the ignorance, or admonish, or let Manolin comment—he instead moves quickly back to the sleeping Santiago, strangely at peace with his pain, the pain which signifies life, dreaming once again of the lions, as Manolin stands watch. We are given Santiago's peace in the envelope of Manolin's concern.

The relationship between Santiago and the marlin has been made much of, and rightly so, for the sense of wonder, the immensity, the brotherhood is beautifully conveyed. But, as the structure and imagery of *The Old Man and the Sea* prove, it is the love between imperfect human beings that lies at the core of Santiago's experience. It is that love that redeems Santiago; and it is that love to which he returns.

Hemingway's Battle with God

Ben Stoltzfus

Ben Stoltzfus argues that *The Old Man and the Sea* is a treatise on Hemingway's rebellion against God. In the following selection, Stoltzfus is careful to point out that Hemingway, the narrator of the tale, and the old man do not hold the same view in the story. It is Hemingway, Stoltzfus argues, who points out that the old man is battling God in the shape of the marlin. The old man remains unaware of the stature of his fight. A two-time Fulbright scholar, Stoltzfus was a professor of literature at the University of California, Riverside. A poet and novelist, he has published articles in many literary journals.

Santiago, the old man of the sea, is a thin, gaunt, wrinkled, and widowed Cuban fisherman who has been fishing the Gulf Stream without a catch for eighty-four consecutive days. The sail of his skiff, like the shirt on his back, whose patches have been faded to many different shades by the sun, looks like "the flag of permanent defeat." Handling heavy fish on the cords has left deep-creased scars on his hands that are as "old as erosions in a fishless desert."

After the first *forty* fishless days Santiago's young helper Manolin, who used to fish with him, was ordered by his parents to go in another boat because the old man was *salao*—"the worst form of unlucky." Santiago is suffering from bad luck, loneliness, old age, and "permanent defeat." With forty as some kind of magical, mysterious, and influential number, Manolin's parents order him to fish in another boat since God seems to have withdrawn His favors from Santiago's skiff.

The biblical resonance of "forty days" and "fishless desert," two early instances of the novel's highly developed Christ motif, leads the reader, subliminally, to associate events in Santi-

Excerpted from *Gide and Hemingway: Rebels Against God*, by Ben Stoltzfus. (Port Washington, NY: Kennikat Press, 1978). Reprinted with the author's permission.

ago's recent past with Christ's sojourn in the wilderness and Moses' forty days on Mount Sinai. Numbers records Israel's wilderness wandering as covering forty years.

Santiago is the victim not only of divine disfavor, but also of social ridicule and pity. Younger fishermen make fun of him while the older ones "speak politely" in his presence of the current and the depths at which they drift their lines. With his bad luck and no fish to sell and no money Santiago must accept food from Martin, the owner of the Terrace. But it is the boy, Manolin, who takes care of him. Since the residents of the village have lost faith in the old man's ability to catch fish they see him perhaps in his final decline. Only Manolin has not lost faith: "'I know you did not leave me because you doubted' [says the old man]. 'It was papa made me leave. I am a boy and I must obey him.' 'I know,' the old man said. 'It is quite normal.' 'He hasn't much faith.' 'No,' the old man said. 'But we have. Haven't we?'"

In spite of his age, Santiago's shoulders and neck are still powerful and strong. His eyes have remained cheerful, confident, and undefeated. His vision is good—better than the vision of younger fishermen who have not gone turtling. If eyes are the mirror of the soul, and the Gulf Stream Hemingway once described in *Green Hills of Africa* is the flow of life itself, then we too should keep faith with this "strange old man" whose eyes are the deep blue color of the Stream, who could once, like a cat or a lion, see in the dark, and who now lives in a shack made with fronds from the royal palm.

While eyes are important in themselves, thematically (much is made of the marlin's eye, shark eyes, cat eyes, a "glimpse of vision," etc.) they serve to highlight the discrepancy between what the villagers see and what Santiago is—between appearance and reality, between what Santiago can still do and what others think he can, between past achievements and present failure. Santiago may seem to be on his last legs, but there is an inner, invisible strength of heroic proportions that will lead him to prove once more that he is still The Champion—*El Campeón.* Thus, one of the themes of *The Old Man and the Sea,* as it was the subject of "The Undefeated," is the gap between outward failure and inner pride, thereby suggesting that point of view is a relevant if not important issue.

Critic Charles K. Hofling, M.D., is of the opinion that the lessening of Santiago's strength due to old age, his loneliness, his ill fortune, his diminished reputation, and his increasing dependence upon the boy, Manolin, are the source of a depression which has affected his self-esteem. Since he was "born to be a fisherman," his sense of identity, his sense of purpose, and his sense of worthwhileness are entirely bound up in his occupational role. Santiago's depression, says Hofling, is the result of shame and narcissistic injury. We might expect other men, less proud than Santiago, to accept the decline that comes with age—to accept the natural and inevitable rhythm of life and death. Santiago apparently will not.

A REBEL AGAINST NATURE

While profoundly attuned to nature's rhythms Santiago is also in rebellion against nature. The fish and the stars are his brothers and while he says he "must kill" the fish, he is glad he does "not have to try to kill the stars," or the moon, or the sun. These are strange thoughts for an old man, thoughts which would seem to imply that if stars were as accessible as fish man would have to try to kill them too. Whatever for? The answer to this question challenges all notions that Santiago is a Christ figure because it implies such extraordinary faith in man's ability to conquer, in man's supremacy, in man's power, in his intelligence, and in his need to assert this manliness. Man takes pleasure in giving death, says Hemingway, because in this way he can usurp one of the godlike attributes. The very need to assimilate such strength and dominion implies pride and pride in turn can lead to rebellion either against nature, or against God, or both. Santiago, for the sake of his pride, is rebelling against old age and death, but Hemingway, through the novel's persona, seems to be challenging the Deity.

Santiago's *pundonor* (a Spanish word meaning honor, probity, courage, self-respect, and pride) makes him "go out too far," kill a marlin, question the notion of "sin," fight "evil" sharks, and return half-dead yet somehow triumphant. Santiago is not just fishing for food. The Christ motif and symbolism are too pronounced, in fact so pronounced that commentators have alluded to the Eucharist, the Crucifixion, and in some cases to a fish-Christ identity. The best commentaries have separated the novel's Christ motif from its pagan message, but for many commentators the christological imagery has tended to obscure its anti-Christian emphasis. This is not to say that Santiago's ordeal and Christ's are not comparable. Hemingway makes it clear that they are. "'Ay,' he [Santiago] said aloud. There is no translation for this word and perhaps it is just a noise such as a man might make, involuntarily, feeling the nail go through his hands and into the wood."

Many other Santiago-Christ associations occur, as, for instance, in the description of the old man's return trip up the hill to his hut. Santiago is carrying the skiff's mast on his back and falls under its weight as Christ fell under the weight of the cross on his way to Calvary. Santiago goes to sleep with his arms outstretched in a cruciform position. Even though he is not yet dead, there are many additional allusions to and symbolic analogies with the Crucifixion. Critic John Halverson mentions the fact that Manolin will bring Santiago a clean shirt, as Joseph of Arimathaea brought clean linen to wrap the body of Christ. Manolin will also bring "stuff from the drugstore" for Santiago's mutilated hands as ointments were brought for the dead Christ. The boy stands watch over the sleeping fisherman as a watch was set over the sepulchre of Christ. . . .

THE MEANING OF THE CHRIST MOTIF

The Christ motif is Hemingway's, not Santiago's (Santiago is blissfully oblivious of it all) and it is essential that we keep this dual point of view in mind. In fact, Hemingway sets Santiago up as a kind of superman rivaling the Deity. Santiago may be killing fish, but Hemingway is killing God. This is why Santiago is not tempted to cut the line and let the big fish go, as Norman Mailer says he should have been, because the despair and pride which drove him too far out in the first place also prompt him to hang on. He would rather die than lose the fish. "You are killing me, fish," says Santiago, but "I do not care who kills who."

Critic John Killinger, in his fine existential study of Hemingway, says that "when God is overthrown and the world is without values, then the rebel must set up his own laws and moral codes." Santiago, from his boyhood onward, has always been self-reliant. He knows the ocean, he knows the weather, and he fishes with precision. The laws and moral code that he observes, except for the perfunctory and ritual use of prayer, are his own and those of the sea. The marlin will teach him dignity, nobility, and endurance, but the law of the sea, and this is the essential point, is survival. Furthermore, Hemingway's precise naturalistic descriptions of life in and on the

Gulf Stream give us more than local color. Man-of-war birds, as well as dolphin, eat the flying fish, turtles eat the men-of-war, while sharks eat the flippers of the sleeping turtles. Sea-hawks eat the little birds and so on and so forth. Santiago, as yet another manifestation of natural forces (and the survival in this case is of the most intelligent), catches and destroys a great sixteen-hundred pound marlin.

The laws of nature are a code in themselves, and man, like the marlin which swims for three days against the Gulf Stream, can, as long as he is alive, resist death and affirm his dignity by "swimming" against the current. There is no point in elaborating Hemingway's "code hero" motif since much has already been written on it, but there is great symbolic value for Hemingway and existentialists alike in "swimming against the current." Santiago, like Sisyphus rolling his stone up the mountain, must affirm his identity as a fisherman (since that is what he was "born for") by fishing and proving it up to the very end. "The thousand times that he had proved it meant nothing. Now he was proving it again. Each time was a new time and he never thought about the past when he was doing it.". . .

Man as King

Santiago performs exceptionally well and all the way under constant pressure. This is his (man's) saving grace, his refusal to give up, his fight to the end. Critic Bernard S. Oldsey sees *The Old Man and the Sea* as a return to the theme of the "undefeated," to the winner takes nothing, the man to whom things happen, the man whom the sharks of the world leave with *nada*. This is what it means to be a man cast adrift in a contingent universe, for who can be more alone than Santiago on the Gulf Stream with no relatives and nothing to return to but his shack in the village? Yet Santiago, the tenacious, precise, and intelligent fisherman, shows what a man can endure, how he can behave, and how he can affirm his identity in the jaws of sharks, adversity, old age, and even death. . . . "I will show them," says Santiago, "what a man can do and what a man endures." Santiago will endure extraordinary privation and suffering to prove that man, of all the beasts, even the lions and the marlins, has the greatest pride and dignity—that man is King.

Santiago's message is that "man can be destroyed but not defeated." Santiago will die, but the example of his heroic

---

AN ENCOUNTER WITH TRUTH

The portrayal of Santiago distinguishes him immediately from the earlier Hemingway heroes in that he is old, thus possessing the accumulated wisdom of a long life and lacking the disrupting physical passions of younger men, although he finds strength in the memory of his youth (dreaming of young lions); and he is humble, while maintaining his pride and dignity. But Santiago's fishing has become singularly unsuccessful and he is in dire need of catching the "big fish." To do so, however, he must go "far out" beyond the "acceptable limits". . . and he must go alone. . . . Thus, the nature of the symbolic quest and the main problem it involves (catching and bringing back the "big fish") are established, as is the dominant tone of confident determination.

With the commencement of the old man's voyage, the rising action of the novel begins. As Santiago rejects convention and goes "far out," the essential symbolism of the work is developed in substantial depth. Thus, as others have noted, the allegorical significance of the land, the sea, the hero, the voyage, the equipment, and the fish are established. With the fading of the land from sight, the first contact with the fish is made and Santiago devotes himself totally to capturing this transcendental object through applying all of the skill, courage, strength, and discipline at his command. He suffers, but he is determined to succeed and, as his portrayal achieves dimension, his fitness for an encounter with this ultimate truth is confirmed. Dramatically, the movement of the rising action is sustained not only by the obvious suspense inherent in the battle but also by the ironic foreshadowing reflected in the hero's voiced anxiety concerning sharks.

William Gifford, *Modern Fiction Studies,* Autumn 1968.

---

struggle will live. To fight heroically is to affirm man's dignity. Critic Stanley Cooperman sees this will to conquer as an echo of the divine but, if I interpret him correctly, only in the sense that Divinity and man's Supreme Will are one and the same. If this is true, then the story of Santiago is a reemphasis and intensification of one of Hemingway's favorite themes: isolation. The individual confronts his own destiny and redeems it by means of a ritual of manhood.

This is not to say that Santiago does not partake of a certain social ethic. Manolin takes care of him and feeds him and the old man is grateful, although, in his fierce pride, he is obviously also resentful, since he plays a game of make-believe with Manolin that will save face and leave his pride intact. Santiago pretends he has yellow rice and fish when

he has none; he pretends he has washed his hands for supper when in fact he has not. This is more than "informed illusion" as one commentator has called it. Santiago must eat,
but he must also protect his ego, and "pretense" is the best
he can come up with. So his decision to go way out on the
eighty-fifth day is a gamble that must pay off. The old man's
injured pride can endure no more and he has to take that
final chance. Critic William J. Handy says that Santiago's decision to go far out is no more than a conscious attempt to
oppose the forces of ill luck and the inevitable demands of a
materialistic society. This is true, but if the argument about
selfhood and pride holds, then Santiago's venture is also a
challenge to man's limitations as well as to the forces of destiny. He is challenging death itself and by extension the
Creator who administers it. Or rather, it is Hemingway who
challenges the Creator since it is he who uses Christian
symbols and it is he who has Santiago slay the fish.

Santiago kills a marlin, but if the Christ motif is more than
comparative, Hemingway is out for bigger game than fish.
Santiago is unaware of the author's symbols even though
Santiago's attitudes and the author's point of view tend to
overlap. Santiago embodies all the virtues of a naturalistic
humanism whereas Hemingway is replacing Christianity
with *pundonor*. While Christ had love and compassion for
the poor and the sinful and the meek and the downtrodden,
Santiago's love for the fish is primarily the respect one develops for the strength and ability of a worthy opponent. He
also feels a love and kinship for all living things including *la
mar*, which is what people call the sea in Spanish when they
love her. But if Santiago's pride is "forced out through the
openings in the sieve of his suffering," it is because he has
met an opponent who is every bit his equal. In spite of the
marlin's size, Santiago wins, and by the time he returns to
port his damaged pride has been restored. Does he not
dream once more of lions? Has he not challenged the stars,
fought sharks, faced death, and brought back a prize? The
marlin's skeleton is the incontrovertible evidence. Few recognize it, least of all the tourists. As Santiago struggles up the
hill to his shack carrying the mast of his "crucifixion" and
collapses on the newspapers with his arms outstretched we
sense that his age and the ordeal have at last destroyed him
physically, but not spiritually.

A METAPHYSICAL REVOLT

Santiago kills fish, in part because he is a fisherman, but also because such acts tend to deny his mortal condition. This is metaphysical revolt, not Christian humility, because it questions the ultimate ends of Creation and protests conditions of mortality imposed on man. The rebel acknowledges yet challenges the power that forces him to live in that condition. Although he defies Creation, Santiago cannot deny it. He cannot suppress Creation, but he can challenge it. He must have the experience of Dominion which can only come through killing. He must continue killing sharks, up to the end, even though he knows it is hopeless, because only in this way can he redeem the initial act of going out "too far" or of "ruining" the marlin or himself. Such desperate heroism is of tragic proportions and relates the old man to Ahab in a way which some commentators have sensed and others denied. Santiago's quest, like Ahab's, is animated by a desire to conquer. Albert Camus says that such an uprising against man's condition "is organized into an over zealous expedition against heaven with the intent of bringing back a prisoner-king whose fall will be proclaimed first, and his death sentence next." "Then when he had seen the fish come out of the water and hang motionless in the sky before he fell, he was sure there was some great *strangeness* [my emphasis] and he could not believe it.". . .

The *pundonor* that prompts bullfighters to challenge death is also at the heart of Santiago's pride. . . . The way Santiago harpoons the marlin demonstrates that he, like any of the celebrated matadors, is a great killer. Hemingway himself was driven by pride and often discoursed on his favorite subjects of bravery and cowardice. He thought of men without inner dignity as an embarrassment. It is not surprising then that he should have created an old man like Santiago whose actions typify and illustrate the values Hemingway holds dear. "You did not kill the fish only to keep alive and to sell for food, he thought. You killed him for pride and because you are a fisherman."

Santiago thinks he feels the fish's heart as he pushes on the harpoon shaft. He is now at the quick of things and the revelation is death. Death is at the heart of life. This is the meaning of the "strange" experience and of his "vision"—inevitable, irreconcilable, and irrevocable death. Death is what gives meaning to life. This, as we have seen, is the theme the existentialists have been stressing and which John Killinger in *Hemingway and the Dead Gods* has written persuasively about. . . .

Santiago is a fisherman, Saint James was a fisherman, and Christ was a "fisher of men." All these people will have suffered in one way or another and Santiago imagines DiMaggio, with his bone spur, to be suffering as much as anyone: "What is a bone spur? he asked himself. *Un espuela de hueso.* We do not have them. Can it be as painful as the spur of a fighting cock in one's heel? I do not think I could endure that." In Spanish *espuela* means not only spur but *spike.* That Santiago's imagination should evoke the image of a fighting cock is significant, since with cock fights, contrary to the "turn the other cheek" of Christianity, it is a fight to the finish. For the reader, however, given the Christ motif, a spike in the foot has its own meaning and again evokes the Crucifixion, an association consonant with popular Spanish religious paintings of the Crucifixion that also frequently depict a cock. Once more Hemingway is using poetic ambiguity. The two themes of the book, the pagan and the Christian, are contained in the same word, *espuela.* Santiago's reaction is a pagan one—the reader's Christian. It is clear that the two themes of the book, and Hemingway's intention in writing it, depend on the necessary distinction between these two points of view.

CHAPTER 2

The Novel's Artistic Accomplishment

READINGS ON
THE OLD MAN AND THE SEA

Excerpt from *A Reader's Guide to Ernest Hemingway*

Arthur Waldhorn

Arthur Waldhorn is the author of *A Reader's Guide to Ernest Hemingway*, from which the following selection is excerpted. In it, Waldhorn argues that Hemingway's genius in *The Old Man and the Sea* lies in its narrative simplicity. Hemingway rarely strays from the straightforward yet lyrical narrative for which he is so well known and appreciated. Throughout this essay, the author compares and contrasts Santiago with several other Hemingway heroes, including Anselmo and Robert Jordan from *For Whom the Bell Tolls*, Harry Morgan from *To Have and Have Not*, Jake Barnes from *The Sun Also Rises*, and Frederic Henry from *A Farewell to Arms*.

Hemingway hooked his first marlin in 1932 in the waters off Havana, twenty years before *The Old Man and the Sea* was published. During those years, Hemingway's enthusiasm for battling these magnificent fish never dulled. Nor did his admiration wane for the Cuban fishermen to whom the marlin was a way of life as well as a livelihood. Among the many fishing articles Hemingway wrote for *Esquire* in the thirties, one told the basic story of *The Old Man and the Sea*. "On the Blue Water: A Gulf Stream Letter," published in 1936, is a short essay that tells about the thrills of marlin-fishing and about an old man alone in his boat when he "hooked a giant marlin that, on the heavy sashcord handline, pulled the skiff far out to sea. Two days later the old man was picked up by fishermen 60 miles to the eastward, the head and forward part of the marlin lashed alongside. What was left of this fish, less than half, weighed eight hundred pounds. The old man had stayed with him a day, a night, a day and another night while the fish swam deep and pulled the boat. When he had come up the old man had pulled the boat up on him and harpooned him. Lashed alongside the sharks had hit him and the old man had fought them out alone in the Gulf Stream in a skiff, clubbing them, stabbing at them, lunging at them with an oar until he was exhausted and the sharks had eaten all that they could hold. He was crying in the boat when the fishermen picked him up, half crazy from his loss, and the sharks were still circling the boat."

Hemingway waited another fifteen years before expanding the essay into a novel, the last printed in his lifetime. The change his hero undergoes from sketch to story is at once apparent. No one brings Santiago home: he steers into harbor alone, dry-eyed and clearheaded. A composite of several actual fishermen Hemingway had known, Santiago has even closer ties with the exemplary heroes of Hemingway's fiction. Like the aging mentors of the bull ring, Juan Belmonte and the "undefeated" Manuel Garcia, and like Anselmo and the other old man at the bridge, Santiago blends humility with pride. Humility is a commodity generally in short supply among Hemingway's heroes, certainly among his apprentices. When their luck (that special Hemingway *mana* that is, even more than chance, an inner fusion of spirit and skill) runs out, pride rather than humility sustains them. Most of Hemingway's younger men are proud of the carefully nurtured discipline that helps them to suppress anxiety. But it is at best a panicky pride and leads easily to flight, or bitterness, or, as with Robert Jordan, a rather shaky metaphysic. Among some of the older men, failed aspirants to exemplary status like Harry Morgan and Richard Cantwell, pride expresses itself as surliness or bravado. Among none of them is humility notable. Santiago has it, though he is too "simple" to know when or how he attained it: he knows only that "it was not disgraceful and it carried no loss of true pride."

THE CONTEST

That part of luck which is happenstance has served Santiago ill for nearly three months. He has caught no fish and lost his apprentice to a luckier boat. Even the furled sail of his skiff looks "like the flag of permanent defeat." Yet the old man's body is strong, his eyes "cheerful and undefeated," his hope and confidence undimmed. "I know many tricks," he says, "and I have resolution." Some of his resolve derives from pride in his skill. No fisherman reads sky and sea with greater assurance; none drops bait straighter or more precisely. "It is better to be lucky," Santiago says. "But I would rather be exact." Like a fine bullfighter, he is methodical, patient, alert, and unshakably determined. Santiago, however, is prouder of being a man than of being an expert, of showing "what a man can do and what a man endures." To be a man is to be like Joe DiMaggio, who plays baseball superbly despite the painful bone spur in his heel. Years earlier, when Santiago and the giant Negro hand-wrestled at Casablanca, they too proved man's grace under pressure. Eyes and hands locked, blood coming from under their fingernails, they struggled sleeplessly for twenty-four hours. Though Santiago wins at last, the Negro— "a fine man and a great athlete"—is not, in the broad sense, beaten.

Neither is the marlin with whom Santiago contends for three days. At the climax of their epic contest, man and fish are as one—exhausted, suffering, but indomitable. As Santiago pulls the fish close enough to harpoon, Hemingway writes, the old man "took all his pain and what was left of his strength *and his long gone pride* and he put it against the fish's agony . . ." [italics added]. Santiago's pride has not deserted him, but it has been transfigured—by wonder, compassion, respect, and love. Together these comprise Santiago's humility, a humility for the most part more convincing than embarrassing, because as [critic] Mark Schorer suggests, it is never self-conscious about granting to things in nature an independence of character as separate as Santiago's. To Santiago, the sea is not merely a place or an enemy but *la mar*, a woman to be loved, however cruel she may be. And she can be cruel, as to the birds who "with their small sad voices are made too delicately for the sea." But she is what she must be, as a man is. It is the same with all living things, whether gentle like the birds and the flying fish, elegant like the green turtle, playful like the lions on the beach, or murderous like the Portuguese man-of-war and the shark. With all creatures, Santiago feels some kinship as well as a humble awareness that "man is not much beside the great birds and beasts."

All that Santiago, like Hemingway, has long sensed intuitively about life comes to dramatic climax during his engagement with the marlin. It is this encounter, as he thinks, that he was born for. After three months of failure, Santiago still rejects rest or compromise. Instead, he elects to risk all by reaching beyond man's reach, by going "too far out." Yet what begins as an act of pride akin to Captain Ahab's in *Moby-Dick* or Kurtz's in *Heart of Darkness* is tempered at once—as soon as the marlin takes the bait—by pity for the creature betrayed by man's intelligence. Man and marlin are inextricably joined by that act, "beyond all people in the world," and, as Santiago thinks, with "no one to help either one of us." As the struggle continues, Santiago's pity turns to respect and at last to love. For a fleeting moment before he kills the marlin, Santiago, purged of all human pride, is willing to die for or with the fish: "Never have I seen a greater, or more beautiful, or a calmer or more noble thing than you, brother. Come on and kill me. I do not care who kills who."

LIVING AND DYING

With that simple lyric cry, Santiago articulates an equally simple but profound truth inherent in *The Old Man and the Sea*. He and the fish are indeed "brothers," as are all creatures trapped in the inescapable process of living and dying. A hook ripping its mouth, the fish endures and struggles for its freedom; a line lacerating his back and hands, the old man fights to deny the marlin its desire. And the sharks beat them both. *The Old Man and the Sea* is not, as Philip Young rightly observes, an allegory about man against nature, but a story about the inevitable doom facing all "joined by the necessity of killing and being killed." Doom is not, in Hemingway's vision, to be identified with defeat. All creatures share doom. Knowing this breeds humility in man, the reverence Santiago feels for the marlin alive and dead. Defeat means yielding to doom without a struggle, abandoning, in effect, the pride that makes it worthwhile to be a man. "You killed him for pride and because you are a fisherman," Santiago says. He kills, then, because not to do so would have meant defeat, and "man is not made for defeat. A man can be destroyed but not defeated."

Once the sharks come to mutilate the fish, Santiago thinks he has violated his luck by going out too far. A natural plaint growing out of physical and spiritual exhaustion, it is not an admission of guilt or sin or even, at last, of regret. Had he not ventured alone in quest of the unknowable, Santiago could not have discovered the grandeur a man may command

> ### A FOLK TALE
> Of the books I have read this year, Hemingway's *The Old Man and the Sea* struck me as the most complete job. Hemingway at his best is unique. He tells a folk tale, but it is a sophisticated folk tale. . . . It has no root in experience or reflection. Hemingway's old man is profoundly original. It deals with fundamentals, the origins. Its form, so elaborately contrived, is yet perfectly suited to the massive shape of a folk theme.
>
> Joyce Cary, *New York Times Book Review*, December 7, 1952.

even in failure. It is humility that leads him to say he has gone out too far. But pride surfaces in the dream that ends the novel as once more Santiago conjures up the lions along the white beaches ("so white they hurt your eyes"). Those persistent memories of his youth—of grace, strength, and purity—have always goaded Santiago to conquer the unconquerable.

Writing to General Lanham about *The Old Man and The Sea*, Hemingway repeated a claim he had made earlier for *Across the River and Into the Trees:* the novel had everything in it he had always believed in. This time, he notes, the difference is that the story is simple and written as simply as he could write it. Insofar as Hemingway stays within the boundaries of simplicity, *The Old Man and the Sea* is superb. For the most part, he does, both thematically and stylistically. The narrative pattern is unexceptionable. Taut, precisely proportioned, the plot never exaggerates suspense or lingers overlong on the (almost literal) dying fall. The cadence and accent of Santiago's Spanish-English are—as in the best passages of *For Whom the Bell Tolls*—at once credible and poignant. Rarely has exposition been more lucid, description more evocative, or both so relevant to emotive and thematic force. Santiago's pride in his craft is delineated with meticulous detail. When he baits a line, "each bait hung head down with the shank of the hook inside the bait fish, tied and sewed solid and all the projecting part of the hook, the curve and the point, was covered with fresh sardines. Each sardine was hooked through both eyes so that they made a half-garland on the projecting steel. There was no part of the hook that a great fish could feel which was not sweet smelling and good tasting." The genius of the exposition shines forth in the final sentence, which—by shifting prose rhythm and vocabulary: "great fish," "sweet smelling," and "good tasting"—wrests the passage from the professional writer and restores it to the professional fisherman.

The noblest passages in *The Old Man and the Sea* work the same magic by centering consistently on Santiago's consciousness and sensibility. When Santiago dexterously guts a tuna or a dolphin for food, it is a hungry, desperate old man we recognize, not Ernest Hemingway fishing from the deck of the *Pilar*. Similarly, in the eloquent descriptions of the sea, it is the concrete sensuality of Santiago's primitive response that makes the essential poetry. He sniffs "the clean early morning smell of the ocean" and feels, through current and wind, changes in the day and night. Visually, he is keenest and most responsive. The hues of the sea, red plankton, yellow Sargasso weed, the purple filaments of the man-of-war, and the lavender stripes of the marlin—all fill the old man with wonder. Yet more wondrous and impressive is the motion of the sea and its creatures. Descriptions of the dip, slant, and dive of a man-of-war bird in pursuit of flying fish or the churning leaps of tuna animate the sense of what indeed Santiago was born for. Caught up in the lithe vitality and sinuous grace of natural movement, he is rhythmically unified with his environment. No abstract commentary can amplify the dimension of Hemingway's simple and dramatic juxtaposition of Santiago's cramped hand ("a treachery of one's own body") against the marlin's first marvelously supple leap.

LITERARY FLAWS

Heminway's virtuosity is not entirely without flaw. Occasionally, an image becomes too sophisticated, too literary, as when the marlin's eye looks "as detached as the mirrors in a periscope or as a saint in a procession." More jarring are those few passages in which significance—religious, poetic, mystical—is force-fed into the narrative. Santiago falls out of character when he reflects upon man's good fortune in not having to kill the sun, moon, or stars, and also when he falters into awkward ecstasy about his "true brothers" in nature. It is not that Santiago, following the tradition of the exemplary hero, should not think. Indeed he does, more than most exemplary heroes do. "Because it is all I have left," he says when the sharks strike. "That and baseball." But baseball, epitomized by Joe DiMaggio (also the son of a fisherman) and his bone spur, inspires in Santiago wholly relevant musings. Santiago's thoughts are compelling at the level of his immediate experience or through memories pertinent to that experience. But when Hemingway imposes abstractions extrinsic to the context, simplicity—the enduring power of the novel—gets mired in self-conscious sophistry.

Fortunately, Hemingway's excesses are few. *The Old Man and the Sea* is, however, baited with choice morsels of symbolism tempting some readers to extravagances of their own. Shortly after the novel was published, Hemingway teased critical imagination with this statement: "I tried to make a real old man, a real boy, a real sea, and a real fish and real shark. But if I make them good and true enough they would mean many things." At once, critics spread their nets far and lowered them deep. Their haul included some indigestible blowfish (like the suggestion that the sharks symbolize critics ravaging the body of Hemingway's work) as well as more substantial fare.

Because the story abounds in religious as well as natural and pantheistic analogies, some critics have read the novel as a Christian allegory. A host of symbols lends support to the hypothesis: Santiago (St. James in English) is, as Carlos Baker writes, a man of "humility, natural piety, and compassion"; he is a fisherman and a teacher (of the young Manolin); the days he lingers at sea agonizing between humility and pride approximate in number those of Christ's sojourn in the desert; his hands are scarred, the mast he carries up the hill resembles the Cross, he assumes the posture (in sleep) of the Crucifixion, and his cry of agony—"Ay"—is, Hemingway writes, "a noise such as a man might make, involuntarily, feeling the nail go through his hands and into the wood"; and, of course, the fish itself is an ancient Christian symbol.

Although Christian symbolism inspirits *The Old Man and the Sea*, the symbols do not transform it into a Christian story or allegory any more than Christian overtones alter the essential humanism of *The Sun Also Rises, A Farewell to Arms*, or *Across the River and Into the Trees*. If there is a crucifixion here, it is a man who is crucified, not a god. And it is a man for whom prayer is a superstitious sop uttered "mechanically" or "automatically," and for whom sin is beyond comprehension or belief. What Santiago dreams about is the strength and fortitude of man, not salvation. But since humanist and

Christian alike share a love for man and compassion for what he must endure, a discreet reading of the symbols may show that the Christian elements serve to reaffirm the humanist theme of struggle and triumph. To force the Christian thesis beyond this point is futile. In fact, some critics have argued cogently that *The Old Man and the Sea* is more like a Greek agon than like a Christian passion. Going too far out is typical of the hero in Greek tragedy, as is his inevitable penalty for *hubris* (in this case, one critic suggests, Nemesis assumes the guise of sharks).

The Old Man and the Sea is a welcome work after the disastrous *Across the River and Into the Trees.* Even a hostile critic might have been less than pleased with so ragged and crabbed an end to a distinguished career of fiction. A short book (Hemingway's only novella), but not a slight one, *The Old Man and the Sea* sounds a muted note of victory for the artist and the man. "It's as though I had gotten finally what I had been working for all my life," Hemingway wrote. What had he been working for? Something more, his novels and stories suggest, than the discipline and moral stamina implicit in the "code"—almost, rather, a disengagement from mortality. Yet death and loneliness persist to the end. Too honest to alter the stark page-face of reality, Hemingway nevertheless glosses the margins. A romantic yearning for renewal—almost for immortality—attends both Hemingway's work and his life. . . . Every hero must, like his creator, confront what he would prefer to ignore. Over the years, however, Hemingway explores paths other than the inevitable way to the insurmountable wall.

THE APPRENTICE

There are many trails, trails the exemplary hero usually avoids, sure they lead at last to the wall. But the apprentice persists, expending much psychic and physical energy on his quest. Jake Barnes, Frederic Henry, and Richard Cantwell survey the road to Christianity but find it impassable. All journey toward a love beyond lust, seeking what Robert Jordan calls "an alliance against death." Always they run into the dead end of mortality. From the thirties onward, the apprentice tries a broader highway where many travel, hoping to reanimate his spirit through the community of men. Again . . . the effort is vain. At last, failing with immediate experience, Hemingway groped beyond it. In his personal life, the result was nostalgia, an attempt to re-create the vitality of the past. In his art, all the early strands of Christianity and love—for nature, women, and all mankind—twine into an elementary transcendentalism, an idealized metaphysic of life within and beyond death, an ordering principle less stringent than the "code" his heroes had always needed to face *nada*. Without abandoning the "code," Hemingway sought to gentle it, to discover perhaps a "separate peace" of renewal and affirmation within the "separate peace" rooted in death and negation.

Until *The Old Man and the Sea*, most of Hemingway's later efforts in this direction failed. Sometimes the hero . . . is falsely placed; sometimes . . . he has too much pride. Only in the symbol of the leopard frozen near the summit of Kilimanjaro does one glimpse the enduring quality Hemingway wished to project as an eternally *living* force. Even Hemingway's style often fails him in the later work, its vitality sapped by straining after eccentric effects. But in *The Old Man and the Sea* Hemingway locates at last the subject, setting, and character appropriate for what he had so long tried to express. Almost as an omen, the style is again sure, its lapses few and never fatal.

The world is still present in *The Old Man and the Sea*, but remote. Only the tourists remind us of society. And they, insensitive still as they were in *The Sun Also Rises*, are unworthy, as Santiago says, to eat the flesh of the fish he catches to feed them. There are no women (except for a photograph of Santiago's wife, removed "because it made him too lonely to see it," and a picture of the Virgin of Cobre), and no men other than the boy Manolin, who appears only before and after Santiago's voyage. A shrunken world, much simplified, it has nonetheless the range of metaphor and the pertinence of parable. All of mortality is here, and courage, and love, and, for the last time, the possibility of renewal. The sea is a vast universe, but although Santiago sails alone, he feels neither isolated nor alienated. To be at one with nature is easier than with a woman or society. Hemingway's apprentices had all known this, but they were too young to forsake what must at last destroy them. Perhaps, then, one must be old and have suffered all in order to survive. But survival is not renewal. A "strange" old man, Santiago knows this and thus must journey on, still seeking an eternal "yes."

Symbolism in *The Old Man and the Sea*

Keiichi Harada

Keiichi Harada points out the primary symbolism in *The Old Man and the Sea*, including the meaning of the ocean, the sharks, the marlin, and other elements. Harada argues that the book works on both allegorical and symbolic as well as narrative levels. Harada is a lecturer in American literature at Aoyama Gakuin University in Tokyo. His works include a Japanese translation of Melville's *Billy Budd*.

What makes that very simple story, *The Old Man and the Sea*, an esthetically satisfying work of art is the fact that Hemingway recognizes the value of "multi-layeredness" of literature as a basis of a "good" and "true" work of art and uses it in his novels. In this novel, he utilizes a great variety of images, symbols, and archetypal patterns which make the novel a rich one and which allow many interpretations.

This short essay is an attempt to develop some of the symbolic images in the novel into their full meanings and thus to see what Hemingway has done in representing a reality.

OF THE OLD MAN AND THE OCEAN

As we know from such great literary works as the *Odyssey*, *Moby-Dick*, or "The Rime of the Ancient Mariner," a great number of writers have used the sea as something that reveals deep realities of man and the universe. It is a place where man's destiny and identity are sought after, dramatized, and clarified. However, these realities are revealed only when man is involved in and participates in the life of the sea. Hemingway also seems to have held such an idea of the sea in composing his masterpiece, *The Old Man and the Sea*. Thus, for Santiago, the ocean is not an objectifiable place for exploitation, as it seems to the younger fishermen,

"The Marlin and the Shark: A Note on *The Old Man and the Sea*," by Keiichi Harada, in *Hemingway and His Critics*, edited by Carlos Baker. Copyright 1961 by Hill and Wang, Inc. Reprinted with the author's permission.

but is considered as a personality, which he considers in terms of femininity. It is feminine because of its wantonness and because it embodies both kindness and cruelty. But more. It is so, because it contains in itself so many elements of fertility and possibility, as many myths of woman demonstrate, as to be deep enough to hide in its depth a never-heard-of or never-seen-of great fish that Santiago eventually meets; wide enough to make it possible for the old man to travel into the region where the unknowable and unknown secrets of reality can be known and experienced; and large enough to allow him to live in eternity. Such a notion of the sea may be more strongly substantiated when we realize that the old man is a lonely figure when he is engaged in the act of fishing. The novel opens with the sentence: "He was an old man who fished alone in a skiff in the Gulf Stream." It is true that the aloneness of Santiago is one forced from the outside by more realistic circumstances: that is, his best and only companion, Manolin, had to leave him because the boy's father decided that the old man, who had not been able to catch any fish for over a month, was *salao*, the worst form of unlucky, and forced the boy to leave him. However, in a deeper level of meaning, it is only natural and logical that the old man should be alone, for, as we shall see more fully later, he has made up his mind to fish "far out" in order to achieve the task "that which he was born for," as he again and again vows in the course of his fishing voyage. For a fisherman of his character, the vow is a serious one, for all his honors and glories as a fisherman depend upon whether he can perform the task perfectly. No matter what kind of suffering and trial he has to go through he has to fulfill his destiny, and thus the act of performing the task becomes a kind of ritual. Each individual has his own sense of destiny and the task should be met by himself and for himself. There is no one else capable of this undertaking or allowed to participate in this ritualistic procedure. It is a sort of esoteric religious rite where the particular individual has to face his holy destiny. In the course of various trials and sufferings, the old man wishes that the boy could be with him to help, but it is not to be permitted, for he alone has to endure the sufferings to fulfill his destiny. Thus, the ocean becomes a place where the old man searches his own identity through the act of pursuing the fish.

OF THE LIONS AND THE BONE SPUR

The most obvious pattern in the structure of the novel is that of the alternation of dream-memory and actual experience. This is also the device, as any reader of Hemingway may notice, that is employed in such a story as "The Snows of Kilimanjaro." This device is generally an attempt to clarify man's present conditions by contrasting the past with the present. The experiences of the past are not meaningless and useless facts but are often "recaptured" by the self through the discriminating and organizing process of the mind in order to establish one's self-identity. Associations and remembrances do not take place at random but are directed toward such an end.

The most recurrent image in the dream of Santiago is that of lions. Whenever he dreams, they almost always appear. Besides, he

> no longer dreamed of storms, nor of women, nor of great occurrences, nor of great fish, nor fights, nor contests of strength, nor of his wife. He only dreamed of places now and of the lions on the beach. They played like young cats in the dusk and he loved them as he loved the boy.

And he wonders why the lions are "the main thing that is left." It is also the question that arises in the mind of the reader. Let alone the Freudian interpretations, we may understand this image in connection with the idea of primitivism, which has been a constant resort of Hemingway from *The Sun Also Rises* onward. The primitive scenes as contrasted to man-made societies in Hemingway's works seem to play the role of a giver of strength and purity. Harry's dream in "The Snows of Kilimanjaro" is a case in point. Among his various dreams, that of the life among the snowy mountains brings forth not only the vitality he once possessed, but also the cleansing power of nature when he remembers that "the snow was so bright it hurt your eyes." In a similar fashion, Santiago dreams of the lions on the beaches of Africa. The long golden beaches and the white beaches are "so white they hurt your eyes." The lions and the whiteness of beaches that live in his happy memories have become part of the personality of the old man and give him a purity to his purpose and sense of vitality that drives him toward the goal "that which he was born for."

Another important image is that of DiMaggio. It does not live in his memories and dreams as the lions do, but it is

fully alive in his consciousness. The old man loves baseball
as some other heroes of Hemingway love bullfighting. In
fact, just as the lions are "the main thing that is left" in his
dreams, so is baseball all he has left when he is on his way
home after a long-endured fight with the fish. And whenever he thinks of baseball, there inevitably appears the figure of DiMaggio. He is a great baseball player and worthy
of the old man's admiration. Santiago feels closer to him
the more because his father was also a fisherman and he
can certainly understand how a fisherman like Santiago
feels. But the most important factor in DiMaggio that at-
tracts the old man's attention is the bone spur that DiMaggio is supposed to have. It is precisely this bone spur that
has made DiMaggio transfigured to something more than a
mere hero. It comes to have a symbolic significance to the
mind of the old man. To him DiMaggio symbolizes a man
who both endures sufferings and achieves greatness. Notice that it is almost always when the old man faces crises
and hard trials that he remembers DiMaggio. He has become not only a source of Santiago's strength and vitality
but also an absolute criterion and directing source of his
action. The old man decides that he "must be worthy of the
great DiMaggio who does all things perfectly even with the
pain of the bone spur in his heel." When he feels weakness
within himself during the long struggle against the great
fish, his mind turns to DiMaggio and he asks himself: "Do
you believe the great DiMaggio would stay with a fish as
long as I will stay with this one?" With an affirmative answer, "I am sure he would," he then goes on fighting with
renewed strength.

This takes us further to another plane of significance in
the novel: the significance of the image of the "bone spur."
The classic analogy of the image is fairly obvious, the tradition of which, I believe, underlies the theme of the novel
in many ways. It reminds us, for instance, of Odysseus'
scar, Achilles' wound, or of one of the anagnorisis scenes
in Sophocles' *Oedipus Tyrannus.* The significance of the
analogy lies: (1) these heroes are all "noble" characters
and do the actions of "proper magnitude," as Aristotle points
out, and (2) the scars on their feet are used to bring about
their own identity in one way or another. . . . It is advisable to
use a loose definition and analogy. . . . Now what strikes the
old man concerning DiMaggio is, as we have seen, that

the latter, despite his pain in his heel, endured the sufferings and achieved greatness. His bone spur is a reminder of the nobleness of an action and of "what a man can do and what a man endures." Thus the image of a hero in his memory and consciousness helps formulate his present identity and discover his possibility.

This fact becomes more significant when we notice that, during his pursuit of the great fish, his hand becomes cramped and his back starts to ache. Whenever he feels that "the hands and the back hurt truly," he remembers DiMaggio's bone spur. Whatever he does, he wishes to follow the example of DiMaggio. His mere past memory of a hero now becomes part of himself. The pain in his hands and back may remind us of the image of Christ, as Professor Carlos Baker points out. But we may not be far wrong to take it that it is a constant reminder to the old man of the limitation of finite human being and thus helps him attain humility by way of the recognition of a classic idea of *hubris*, the point of which we shall discuss in our next section.

OF THE MARLIN AND THE SHARK

When Santiago declared that he would go "far out," he felt "confident" because the day was the eighty-fifth day and it meant to his mind a lucky day. The prospect of the day seemed to be a smiling one. Far out in the sea, he finally succeeds in hooking the great fish. But it is not until he has been taken farther out on the ocean by the fish that he realizes how big the fish is. He has never "seen a greater, or more beautiful, or a calmer or more noble thing than" this fish. As he continues his fight, his respect for the greatness and dignity of the fish increases. He loves the fish as if it were his own brother, and yet he is determined to kill him. This determination and subsequent actions of his come from his sense of destiny. This decision is founded on his firm feeling that he is to show "what a man can do and what a man endures" and to fulfill the task "that which he was born for."

At this point, it may be helpful to notice two phases of time structure in the old man's consciousness. His being a fisherman is predetermined, so to speak, as far as we are made known of him in the novel. But, on the other hand, what saves him from being a mere victim of the past and making predetermination is what may be called his existential time consciousness. In the early stage of his fishing voyage, he shows a defiance to a deterministic and fatalistic attitude. His failure of catching fish for the past eighty-four days casts a doubt on his confidence. This doubt makes him say, "Only I have no luck any more." If it is true, it would be a fatal blow to a fisherman. But then he immediately rejects such a notion and tells himself, "But who knows? Maybe today. Every day is a new day." Again, when he recognizes the "greatness and glory" of the fish, his determination to kill him is strengthened the more for it. Hemingway describes the mind of Santiago at this moment as follows:

> "I told the boy I was a strange old man," he said. "Now is when I must prove it." The thousand times that he had proved it meant nothing.

> Now he was proving it again. *Each time was a new time and he never thought about the past when he was doing it* (italics are mine).

The characteristic of this kind of pursuit, as Professor Hans Meyerhoff points out, "enables the individual to live within the dimension of a permanent 'now,' without past or future." Thus we see Santiago, in his pursuit of the fish, being given vitality and driven by the image of the lions and DiMaggio, and, at the same time, freed from any deterministic sense of the past and united to a permanent "now."

As the story proceeds, the real issue of Santiago's pursuit becomes clearer. The fish he has hooked ceases to be a mere physical object. It comes to symbolize something which belongs to a different realm of existence. This is a wholly new experience for the old man in his long years of life as a fisherman. Until he faces this fish, he has never seen or heard of such a great and beautiful fish. And he feels that "there is no one worthy of eating him from the manner of his behavior and his great dignity." The old man's wisdom and long years of experience prove to be useless, because the experience is a *Begegnung* with something which transcends the "limit-situation" of a physical and temporal being which is necessarily bound by finitude and time. This is precisely the reason why the old man repeatedly expresses his desire to share the fate with the fish. What the image of DiMaggio does to him in his memory and consciousness, the fish does in actuality. He feels he is not "worthy of eating him," but nevertheless he tries to kill him. He has to kill him because it is a kind of sacrifice to complete the ritual, and the sacrifice is absolutely necessary to attain a rebirth through death.

Either one of them has to die for that purpose. Or possibly both. Thus he cries, "Come on and kill me, I do not care who kills who," and later, "If I were towing him behind there would be no question. Nor if the fish were in the skiff, with all dignity gone, there would be no question either . . . let him bring me in if it pleases him. I am only better than him through trickery. . . ." As these words of the old man show, Santiago's pursuit has now become a quest: a quest for the union with the transcendental, that he nor anyone else has ever seen or ever been able to see. Now it makes no difference which one dies as long as he succeeds in the quest. He does succeed. The pursuer and the pursued have become one. Temporality is united with eternity.

But the fact remains that Santiago belongs to the temporal order of time. He has to pay the price for what he has done and for what he got. Already, at the beginning of the novel, we seem to discern a tragic flaw when he tells the boy that he intends to go "far out" to fish. The region where he hooked the great fish is that where no other fishermen can be seen, or, more symbolically, understood, where no earthly being is permitted to enter. Whether he has committed the act consciously or not matters little. He has overstepped the boundary of man's finite and limited nature. The act may be interpreted more as a *hubris* than as a sin. For the concept of sin in a Christian context involves some conscious act or motivation, while *hubris* does not necessarily have to do with it. For example, we may argue that the Moira was too severe on Oedipus for he has really nothing to do with the making of his own fate. But just the same, it is a *hubris*, and he has to take the responsibility. Indeed, that the old man has gone "too far out" is partly the responsibility of the fish that has towed the fishing boat and Santiago toward the heart of the ocean. And that he killed the fish thus "far out" on the sea comes from a clear and simple reason, not wholly his own responsibility that he was born a fisherman and nothing else, the fact of which he cannot help himself. But just the same, he has to pay the price for the glory. In this twentieth-century novel, the Nemesis takes the shape of the sharks. After he has achieved the act of greatness, the union with the eternal and the transcendental, he turns his boat toward the land, the home of temporality, futility, and fixedness. It is then that the old man has to face a great enemy, the sharks. Just like the Furies haunting the doomed

Orestes, the sharks seem to be determined to prevent the old man from taking the prize of his fighting out of the sacred region. It is as if these sharks were the mortuary divinities who are angered by the sacrilegious attempt of the old man to expose the unknowable face to those in the temporary and finite order. That exhilarated joy of the old man was something attained by his plunging into the abyss of an eternal "now." But after the moment of this exhilaration, the old man is reminded of his actual predicament. He lives in time. And the goal of time is death and destruction. The sharks are the symbol of "time." They are the incarnation of "Devouring Time," and Santiago finally learns, with Shakespeare, that "nothing 'gainst Time's scythe can make defense" (Sonnet XII). He is now forced to learn the reality of man's existence. He says to the fish, "I shouldn't have gone out so far, fish, neither for you nor for me, I'm sorry, fish." He recognizes that he has transgressed his limitation, that he has to meet the consequences of his *hubris.* Now, at last, he would have admitted to the full the truth of the lesson of the *Oresteia,* that "By suffering man learns."

However, he is not "defeated," despite the fact that he has been "beaten," as he himself admits, by his violation of the sacred code. He pronounces that "nothing" beat him really and that his only fault was that he "went out too far." It is because he has learned "by suffering," and he now *knows* the truth that the penalty of his *hubris* is the loss of his supreme identity in an eternal order. . . . Santiago has learned much in a few days of fishing voyage through much suffering, and he is now able to pronounce a judgment upon the inscrutable human existence and man's destiny: he has "gone too far out." His failure has thus turned out to be his victory.

Hemingway's Religious Symbolism

Joseph Waldmeir

Joseph Waldmeir, member of the Department of American Thought and Language at Michigan State University, argues that the religious symbolism in *The Old Man and the Sea*, while superficially Christian, is based on nature. Hemingway's religion, Waldmeir contends, "does not extend beyond the limits of this world."

In recent years, critics have become increasingly suspicious that it is necessary to read Ernest Hemingway's work on the symbolic as well as on the story level in order to gain a full appreciation of its art. Since the publication of *The Old Man and the Sea*, the suspicion has become first an awareness, then a certainty. Of all Hemingway's work, this one demands most to be read on both levels; and the story, its details, its method of presentation, are sufficiently similar to the balance of his work as to suggest strongly the possibility of a similar reading and perhaps a similar interpretation.

The Old Man and the Sea is, as story, very good Hemingway. It is swiftly and smoothly told; the conflict is resolved into a struggle between a man and a force which he scarcely comprehends, but which he knows that he must continue to strive against, though knowing too that the struggle must end in defeat. The defeat is only apparent, however, for, as in "The Undefeated," it becomes increasingly clear throughout the story that it is not victory or defeat that matters but the struggle itself. Furthermore, *The Old Man and the Sea*, while reasserting the set of values, the philosophy which permeates all of Hemingway, is built upon the great abstractions—love and truth and honor and loyalty and pride and humility—and again speaks of the proper method of attaining and retaining these virtues, and of the spiritual satisfaction in-

Joseph Waldmeir, "*Confiteor Hominem:* Ernest Hemingway's Religion of Man." *Papers of the Michigan Academy of Science, Arts, and Letters*, XLII, pp. 349–56. Reprinted by permission of the University of Michigan Press.

evitably bestowed upon their holder.

The Christian religious symbols running through the story, which are so closely interwoven with the story in fact as to suggest an allegorical intention on Hemingway's part, are so obvious as to require little more than a listing of them here. The Old Man is a fisherman, and he is also a teacher, one who has taught the boy not only how to fish—that is, how to make a living—but how to behave as well, giving him the pride and humility necessary to a good life. During the trials with the great fish and with the sharks his hands pain him terribly, his back is lashed by the line, he gets an eye-piercing headache, and his chest constricts and he spits blood. He hooks the fish at noon, and at noon of the third day he kills it by driving his harpoon into its heart. As he sees the second and third sharks attacking, the Old Man calls aloud "'Ay,'" and Hemingway comments: "There is no translation for this word and perhaps it is just such a noise as a man might make, involuntarily, feeling the nail go through his hand and into the wood." On landing, the Old Man shoulders his mast and goes upward from the sea toward his hut; he is forced to rest several times on his journey up the hill, and when he reaches the hut he lies on the bed "with his arms out straight and the palms of his hands up."

THE FISH AS CHRISTIAN SYMBOL

The Christian symbolism so evident here shifts from man to fish—a legitimate symbol for Christ since the beginning of Christianity, as it was a legitimate religious symbol before Christianity—and back to man throughout the story. This apparent confusion is consistent not only within the Hemingway philosophy as an example of the sacrificer-sacrificed phenomenon (a point which I will discuss later in this paper) but within formal Christianity as well, if the doctrine of the Trinity be accepted. Furthermore, the phenomenon itself closely parallels the Roman Catholic sacrifice of the Mass, wherein a fusion of the priest-man with Christ takes place at the moment of Transubstantiation.

Along with the Christ symbols, reinforcing them, but depending on them for its importance, is a rather intricate numerology. It is not formalized—neither is the numerology of Christianity—but it is carefully set forth.

Three, seven, and forty are key numbers in the Old and New Testaments, and in the religion, and Hemingway makes a judicious use of them. The Old Man, as the story opens, has fished alone for forty-four famine days and with the boy for forty more. The Old Man's trial with the great fish lasts exactly three days; the fish is landed on the seventh attempt; seven sharks are killed; and, although Christ fell only three times under the Cross, whereas the Old Man has to rest from the weight of the mast seven times, there is a consistency in the equal importance of the numbers themselves.

But, once it has been established that *The Old Man and the Sea* may be read on the symbolic as well as on the story level, a new problem presents itself, a problem which grows out of the nature of the symbolic level and out of the disturbing realization that the two levels exist harmoniously in the work. I think that the problem may best be expressed by two questions which the discerning reader must have asked himself as he put *The Old Man and the Sea* down: Is the story as it appears at first glance to be, a Christian allegory? Has the old master tough guy decided, in the words of Colonel Cantwell, "to run as a Christian"? If neither of these questions can be answered with an unqualified affirmative—and I submit that they cannot—then a further question must be asked: Just what is the book's message?

The answer assumes a third level on which *The Old Man and the Sea* must be read—as a sort of allegorical commentary by the author on all his previous work, by means of which it may be established that the religious overtones of *The Old Man and the Sea* are not peculiar to that book among Hemingway's works, and that Hemingway has finally taken the decisive step in elevating what might be called his philosophy of Manhood to the level of a religion.

Two aspects of the total work, including *The Old Man and the Sea*, must be considered at this point in order to clarify the above conclusion on the one hand, and to answer the questions concerning Hemingway's Christianity on the other.

The first of these aspects is Hemingway's concern with man as man, with man in his relation to things of this world almost exclusively. The other world, God, does not often enter into the thoughts, plans, or emotions of a Hemingway character. God exists—most of the characters are willing to admit His existence, or at least, unwilling to deny it—but not as an immanent Being, not ever benevolent or malevolent.

God is sometimes prayed to by the Hemingway hero at

moments of crisis, but His aid or succor are never depended upon, never really expected. Thus we have Jake Barnes in the Cathedral at Pamplona, on the eve of his great trial, praying for everybody he can think of, for good bullfights and good fishing; and as he becomes aware of himself kneeling, head bent, he

> was a little ashamed, and regretted that I was such a rotten Catholic, but realized that there was nothing I could do about it, at least for awhile, and maybe never, but that anyway it was a grand religion, and I only wished I felt religious and maybe I would the next time.

And thus, too, we have the Old Man, who, after twenty-four hours of his monumental struggle have passed, prays for heavenly assistance mechanically, automatically, thinking, "I am not religious," and "Hail Marys are easier to say than Our Fathers." And after forty-five hours, he says:

> "Now that I have him coming so beautifully, God help me to endure. I'll say a hundred Our Fathers and a hundred Hail Marys. But I cannot say them now."
>
> Consider them said, he thought, I'll say them later.

But when the struggle is ended and the full ironic impact of his "victory" is clear, he asks himself what it was that beat him, and answers, "Nothing . . . I went out too far."

He who depends too heavily on prayer, or for that matter on any external aids when faced with a crisis, is not very admirable to Hemingway. In *Death in the Afternoon,* when he wants to describe the unmanliness of a "cowardly bullfighter" girding himself for action, Hemingway places him in church

> in his bullfighting clothes to pray before the fight, sweating under the armpits, praying that the bull will embiste, that is charge frankly and follow the cloth well; oh blessed Virgin that thou wilt give me a bull that will embiste well, blessed Virgin give me this bull, blessed Virgin, that I should touch this bull in Madrid to-day on a day without wind; promising something of value or a pilgrimage, praying for luck, frightened sick.

A man must depend upon himself alone in order to assert his manhood, and the assertion of his manhood, in the face of insuperable obstacles, is the complete end and justification of his existence for a Hemingway hero. The Old Man *must* endure his useless struggle with the sharks; Manuel, in "The Undefeated," *must,* in spite of his broken wrist and a terrible goring, go in on the bull six times and accept the horn at last; Jake *must* continue to live as "well" and "truly" and "honestly" as he is able in spite of his overwhelming frustration. And each must face his struggle alone, with no recourse to otherworldly help, for only as solitary individuals can they assert their manhood.

And significantly they must go it alone without regard to otherworldly blame. As far as sin is concerned, Jake would probably say along with the Old Man, "Do not think about sin. It is much too late for that and there are people who are paid to do it. Let them think about it." And Manuel would probably nod agreement.

A RIGID SET OF RULES

However, in spite of such obvious rejections of otherworldly Christianity in his affirmation of Manhood, Hemingway has formulated as rigid a set of rules for living and for the attainment of Manhood as can be found in any religion. These rules, along with the detailed procedure for their application, constitute the second aspect of Hemingway's total work to be considered in this paper.

The rules are built upon the great abstractions mentioned above. They are so bound up with the procedure for their application that the procedure itself might be considered to be a rule—or better, that neither rules nor procedure exist without one another. Hemingway's philosophy of Manhood is a philosophy of action; a man is honest when he acts honestly, he is humble when he acts humbly, he loves when he is loving or being loved. Thus, taking an awareness of the rules as he has taken an awareness of the abstractions for granted, Hemingway concerns himself primarily with the presentation of procedure. The procedure is carefully outlined; it is meticulously detailed. If no part of it is overlooked or sloughed off, it must result in a satisfying experience almost in and of itself. . . .

HEMINGWAY'S RELIGION

War, the prize ring, fishing, hunting, and making love are some of the other celebrations by means of which Hemingway's religio-philosophy of Man is conveyed. But the bullfight is the greatest because, besides possessing, as the others do also, a procedure inviolate, intimately related to the great abstractions, it always ends in death. It assumes the stature of a religious sacrifice by means of which a man can place himself in harmony with the universe, can satisfy the spiritual as well as the physical side of his nature, can atone for the grievous omissions and commissions of his past, can purify and elevate himself in much the same way that he can in any sacrificial religion. The difference between Hemingway's religion of man and formal religion is simply—yet profoundly—that in the former the elevation does not extend beyond the limits of this world, and in the latter, Christianity for example, the ultimate elevation is totally otherworldly. . . .

There must be a cognizance of death both from the standpoint of killing and from that of being killed; there must be more than a cognizance actually; there must be an acceptance. Knowledge of death's inevitability so that he does not react to its immediacy, coupled with unconcern for the possibilities of life after death, are necessary attributes of the ideal bullfighter. His aim can extend no further than the great abstractions themselves, how he earns them and how he communicates them. He must realize that it is not *that* one dies but *how* one dies that is important. And equally important, that it is not *that* one kills but *how* one kills. . . .

The abstractions, the rules, the ritual, the sacrifice dominate the details of *The Old Man and the Sea* as they dominate those of "The Undefeated" and *The Sun Also Rises*. We are told carefully, painstakingly, how the Old Man performs his function as fisherman; how he prepares for the hoped-for struggle:

> Before it was really light he had his baits out and was drifting with the current. One bait was down forty fathoms. The second was at seventy-five and the third and fourth were down in the blue water at one hundred and one hundred and twenty-five fathoms. Each bait hung head down with the shank of the hook inside the bait fish, tied and sewed solid and all the projecting part of the hook, the curve and the point, was covered with fresh sardines. Each sardine was hooked through both eyes so that they made a half-garland on the projecting steel.
>
> . . . Each line, as thick around as a big pencil, was looped onto a green-sapped stick so that any pull or touch on the bait would make the stick dip and each line had two forty-fathom coils which could be made fast to the other spare coils so that, if it were necessary, a fish could take out over three hundred fathoms of line.

We are told how he hooks the fish and secures the line, waiting suspensefully for the fish to turn and swallow the bait, then waiting again until it has eaten it well, then striking, "with all the strength of his arms and the pivoted weight of his body," three times, setting the hook; then placing the line across his back and shoulders so that there will be something to give when the fish lunges, and the line will not break. We are told specifically, in terms reminiscent of such descriptions of the bullfight, how the kill is made:

> The old man dropped the line and put his foot on it and lifted the harpoon as high as he could and drove it down with all his strength, and more strength he had just summoned, into the fish's side just behind the great chest fin that rose high in the air to the altitude of a man's chest. He felt the iron go in and he leaned on it and drove it further and then pushed all his weight after it.

The immanence of death for the sacrificer as well as for the sacrificed, and his total disregard of its possibility, are made clear at the climax of the struggle when the Old Man thinks: "You are killing me, fish. . . . Come on and kill me. I do not care who kills who."

A SUPERFICIAL CHRISTIANITY

It is at this point I think that the questions asked earlier in this paper can be answered. Has Hemingway decided to "run as a Christian"? I think not; the evidence in *The Old Man and the Sea*, with the exception of the Christian symbolism, indicates that he is no more Christian now than he was when he wrote *The Sun Also Rises*. But the Christian symbolism *is* in the book, and it *does* appear to constitute a Christian religious allegory. Yes, but on a superficial level. The religious allegory, attached to the two aspects of the total body of Hemingway's work as they appear in *The Old Man and the Sea*, which have been the subject of most of my discussion thus far, actually constitute a third level on which *The Old Man and the Sea* must be read—as the allegorical interpretation of the total body of the work.

I said above that Hemingway is no more Christian now than he was thirty years ago; it has been my intention in this paper to show that he was *no less religious* thirty years ago than he is now. The evidence which I have presented adds up to something more than a philosophy or an ethic, the two terms which have most often been used to describe Hemingway's world view; it adds up to what I would call a Religion of Man. Hemingway did not turn religious to write *The*

Old Man and the Sea. He has always been religious, though his religion is not of the orthodox, organized variety. He celebrates, he has always celebrated, the Religion of Man; *The Old Man and the Sea* merely celebrates it more forcefully and convincingly than any previous Hemingway work. It is the final step in the celebration. It is the book which, on the one hand, elevates the philosophy to a religion by the use of allegory, and on the other, by being an allegory of the total body of his work, enables us to see that work finally from the point of view of religion.

Biblical Allusions in *The Old Man and the Sea*

Joseph M. Flora

Joseph M. Flora was associate professor of English at the University of North Carolina at Chapel Hill when he wrote the following selection. He is the author of books on authors Vardis Fisher and William Ernest Henley as well as numerous published critical essays. Here, Flora traces the biblical allusions found in The Old Man and the Sea *to prove his case that the old man is a Christian who adheres to a "practical Christianity": living one's life in adherence to certain Christian principles.*

From the beginning of his career to the end, Ernest Hemingway made important use of the Bible in his fiction. Critics of "The Old Man and the Sea" have long been aware of biblical cadences and parallels. However, no one has commented on two important biblical passages that Hemingway appears to have used with great deliberation in "The Old Man." Attention to one of these is useful for resolving a controversy about the protagonist; attention to both helps to clarify Hemingway's theme.

One critical disagreement over the work surrounds the question of whether Santiago went "too far out" and thus sinned. Several references to going far out sandwich the central story of the fishing episode. Early in the story, Santiago informs the boy, Manolin, that he is going "far out," where most of the fishermen do not like to go. Hemingway repeats the phrase with some variation, creating a certain biblical cadence thereby. After the devastation of his great fish by the sharks, Santiago brings the earlier determination to go "far out" back to mind as he accuses himself repeatedly: "I shouldn't have gone out so far, fish." His final words before he comes into harbor are put in the same terms: "And what beat you, he thought. 'Nothing,' he said aloud. 'I went out too far.'"

Joseph M. Flora, "Biblical Allusion in *The Old Man and the Sea*," *Studies in Short Fiction*, vol. 10 (1973), pp. 143–47. Copyright 1973 by Newberry College. Reprinted with permission.

His final statement has a simplicity that negates his earlier judgement that he had sinned in killing the marlin. By the careful framing of his story in terms of going far out, Hemingway is, I think, doing something quite different from calling the old man to appreciate the community ashore, as some critics have thought. Rather, by repetition of "far out," Hemingway calls to mind a specific Christian challenge in terms of a New Testament account of Jesus. Santiago's name (Spanish for Saint James) reminds us that Hemingway named his protagonist for one of the twelve disciples, most of whom were fishermen. Saint Luke records the story of the calling of these men in terms that bear important similarities to Hemingway's tale. On a certain day Simon Peter and his fellow fishermen had also had a time of fishing with "no luck." Jesus had been preaching from Peter's boat to a crowd on the shores of Lake Gennesaret:

> Now when he had left speaking, he said unto Simon, Launch out into the deep, and let down your nets for a draught.
> And Simon answering said unto him, Master, we have toiled all the night, and have taken nothing: nevertheless at thy word I will let down the net.
> And when they had this done, they inclosed a great multitude of fishes; and their net brake.
> And they beckoned unto their partners, which were in the other ship, that they should come and help them. And they came, and filled both the ships, so that they began to sink.
> When Simon Peter saw it, he fell down at Jesus' knees, saying Depart from me; for I am a sinful man, O Lord.
> For he was astonished, and all that were with him, at the draught of the fishes which they had taken:
> And so was James, and John, the sons of Zebedee, which were partners with Simon. And Jesus said unto Simon, Fear not: From henceforth thou shalt catch men.
> And when they had brought their ships to land, they forsook all, and followed him.
>
> (Luke 5:4–11)

There is not, of course, a one-to-one parallel between this account and the events of "The Old Man and the Sea." Hemingway was not that kind of writer. Nevertheless, it does not seem unlikely that having named his protagonist for one of the men involved, Hemingway looked again at this story, itself a memorable parable of the Christian calling—full of challenge and promise: "Launch out into the deep." To make the big catch it is necessary to reject the easy and to go "far out."

Appropriately, the twentieth-century Santiago is alone as he accepts the challenge of the Master. Not even Manolin can go with him. By himself he must do "the thing that I was born for." He is also on a larger body of water which has threats greater than those from Gennesaret, but this too is appropriate for the image of the modern Santiago. His need also seems more urgent. In Luke's account, the fishermen were at most tired and discouraged after a fruitless night's work. But Santiago has gone eighty-four days without success. He is old (again unlike James of Luke's Story), and his skiff reflects what life had done to him: "The sail was patched with flour sacks and, furled, it looked like the flag of permanent defeat." But to such men, Christianity has always promised victory with the challenge of launching out into the deep. Ironically, the victory in both Luke's account and Hemingway's makes the characters more humble. Simon Peter, apparently speaking for the other disciples as well, says, "I am a sinful man." Santiago takes a similarly humble position: "If you love him, it is not a sin to kill him. Or is it more?" But in neither case is the sinning or not sinning the point.

SANTIAGO AND CHRIST

By emphasizing Santiago's role as one who accepts the challenge of Jesus, we guard against making too much of the parallel at the end of the novella between Santiago and Jesus. It is true that we are pointedly reminded of Jesus' crucifixion at the end of the work, but this likeness should be seen in terms of discipleship. Santiago becomes more like the Christ because he has dared to launch out into the deep. He thereby experiences tremendous victory—but also great loss. "The Old Man and the Sea" is a striking illustration of what is probably one of Frederic Henry's best thoughts in *A Farewell to Arms*: "It is in defeat that we become Christian." Significantly, the young priest of that novel fails to grasp the truth of Frederic's observation. The Church does not give to Hemingway's characters the direction many of them crave. The story of Santiago is an ironic counterpoint to the story of Simon Peter and the other fishermen. It is not that Christianity is irrelevant to man's needs; it is just that Hemingway came increasingly to believe that man must do what he can do alone.

In addition to counterpointing the action of his story with the biblical account of the fishermen, Hemingway has skillfully produced a verbal texture that recalls one of the most famous of New Testament passages, St. Paul's treatise on love in 1 Corinthians, Chapter 13. The chapter concludes: "And now abideth faith, hope, charity, these three; but the greatest of these is charity." Hemingway has Santiago cherish the same triumvirate and in the same order. Almost immediately Hemingway presents Santiago and the boy together as an embodiment of faith. Speaking of his father, Manolin says, "'He hasn't much faith.' 'No,' the old man said, 'But we have. Haven't we?' 'Yes,' the boy said." Both the boy's and Santiago's dreams of lions in Africa symbolize this faith. As faith moves into the realm of action, hope becomes an important element. About the hope so necessary in pursuit Hemingway observes of Santiago as the old man prepares for his trip: "His hope and his confidence had never gone. But now they were freshening as when the breeze rises." Later the sharks sorely try that hope, but Santiago thinks of the great DiMaggio, who with his painful bone spur that has hampered his baseball playing serves to symbolize the hope active in conflict. So Santiago rallies: "He watched only the forward part of the fish and some of his hope returned." "It is silly not to hope, he thought. Besides I believe it is a sin."

THE THEME OF LOVE

Santiago is a compelling character because with his faith and hope, love is closely interwoven: "most people are heartless about turtles because a turtle's heart will beat for hours after he has been cut up and butchered. But the old man thought, I have such a heart too and my feet and hands are like theirs." Already an important part of the old man, love emerges as the growing part of him, the part that is deepened in the climactic death of the marlin. Santiago's love for the fish is established early: "Fish," he said, "I love you and respect you very much. But I will kill you dead before this day ends." The fish possesses precisely the virtues of Santiago himself, and in the struggle Santiago achieves an at-one-ment with his "victim"; "Never have I seen a greater, or more beautiful, or a calmer or more noble thing than you, brother. Come and kill me. I do not care who kills who." Time is arrested in love as the fish ("which is my brother") dies: "Then the fish came alive, with his death in him, and rose high out of the water showing all his great length and width and all his power and his beauty. He seemed to hang in the air above the old man in the skiff. Then he fell into the water with a crash that sent spray over the old man and over all the skiff." As he prepares to take the fish ashore, Santiago reflects: "I think I felt his heart."

In "The Old Man and the Sea" Hemingway presents a parable of practical Christianity. The theology of Christianity may no longer be valid, but—as Santiago's life illustrates—a practical Christian experience may yet be the best course open to man. To be humble, to endure, to launch out into the deep, to have faith, hope, and love—these achievements are still the most rewarding. "The Old Man and the Sea" illustrates the essence of Christian discipleship and does so in specifically biblical terms.

A Lack of Realism Mars *The Old Man and the Sea*

Robert P. Weeks

In the following article, Robert P. Weeks argues that in *The Old Man and the Sea* Ernest Hemingway does not write with the usual realism to which he adheres in other works. On the contrary, Weeks contends, the novel continually tests the reader's patience with unbelievable coincidences and exaggerations. Weeks is professor of English at the College of Engineering at the University of Michigan. He is the author of several essays on Hemingway.

From the vignettes and stories of his first book, *In Our Time*, to his last, *The Old Man and the Sea*, Ernest Hemingway repeatedly made skillful use of animals to epitomize the subjective state or the situation of his characters. Nick Adams' trout holding itself steady against the cold current of the Big Two-Hearted River, Francis Macomber's gut-shot lion standing off death in the tall grass, the huge, filthy vultures keeping a death-watch on Harry [in *The Snows of Kilimanjaro*] on the plains at the foot of Kilimanjaro—objectively and precisely epitomize the crisis confronting the protagonist in each of these stories.

Yet these animals, and the others Hemingway uses to perform the same function, are nonetheless marvelously real. They possess in abundance . . . solidity of specification: they move, sound, and look like real animals.

The difference, however, in the effectiveness with which Hemingway employs this characteristic device in his best work and in *The Old Man and the Sea* is illuminating. The work of fiction in which Hemingway devoted the most attention to natural objects, *The Old Man and the Sea*, is pieced out with an extraordinary quantity of fakery, extraordinary because one would expect to find no inexactness, no

Robert P. Weeks, "Fakery in *The Old Man and the Sea*," *College English*, December 1962, pp. 188–92.

romanticizing of natural objects in a writer who loathed W.H. Hudson, could not read Thoreau, deplored Melville's rhetoric in *Moby-Dick*, and who was himself criticized by other writers, notably Faulkner, for his devotion to the facts and his unwillingness to "invent."

Santiago, the only human being in the story, is himself depicted as a natural phenomenon, a strange old man whose heart beats like a turtle's, whose "feet and hands are like theirs," whose eyes are "the same color as the sea" and with which he could once "see quite well in the dark. Not in the absolute dark. But almost as a cat sees." But even these natural affinities do not prepare us for what this strange old man can do. As he sits in his skiff with more than six hundred feet of heavy line—the thickness of a pencil—slanting steeply down into the darkness of the stream, Santiago feels a fish nibble at the bait.

> He felt no strain nor weight and he held the line lightly. Then it came again. This time it was a tentative pull, not solid nor heavy, and he knew exactly what it was. One hundred fathoms down a marlin was eating the sardines that covered the point and the shank of the hook where the hand-forged hook projected from the head of the small tuna.

This is not fishing skill; it's clairvoyance. The signals that can be transmitted over a pencil-thick line dangling more than six hundred feet into the ocean are relatively gross. Moreover, as Hemingway himself points out in his essay "Marlin Off Cuba," in *American Big Game Fishing*, published in an elegant limited edition of 906 copies by the Derrydale Press in 1935, one cannot tell whether the fish taking his bait is a marlin or a broadbill for they "take the bait in much the same manner, first, perhaps picking off a few of the sardines with which the point of the hook is covered, then seizing the whole fish used as bait between their jaws to crush it a moment before swallowing it."

THE SHARK FIGHT

This hint that Hemingway may be padding his characterization of Santiago by means of fakery is abundantly confirmed by the action that follows. His combat with the fish is an ordeal that would do in even a vigorous young man. He is at sea nearly three full days, almost all of that time without sleep and during much of it hanging onto a 1,500 pound fish that steadily tows him and his boat for miles, most of it *against* the current of the Gulf Stream. At noon on the third day, the giant fish circles the boat and the old man harpoons it, lashes it to the boat, and sets sail for home. Almost at once the sharks attack the fish, and the old man attacks the sharks. He battles them for more than twelve hours, quitting only when he runs out of weapons. Then, competently—and evidently without sleeping—he sails his little skiff for his home port, arriving shortly before dawn.

The extent to which this is an incredible performance is made clear when we turn to Hemingway himself for some notion of how an actual old Cuban fisherman behaved under similar circumstances. In "On the Blue Water," an essay that appeared in *Esquire* in 1936, Hemingway described how an old Cuban fisherman out in the Atlantic alone had been towed sixty miles to sea by a large marlin. When he was picked up by fishermen two days later with the marlin lashed to his small boat, the old man was weeping, half-demented, and sharks circled his boat.

It is hardly surprising that Santiago's clairvoyancy also enables him to be an uncanny meteorologist. While he is being towed by his fish, he looks at the sky, then soliloquizes: "If there is a hurricane you always see the signs of it in the sky for days ahead, if you are at sea. They do not see it ashore because they do not know what to look for." Scientists on land, sea, and in the air equipped with delicate pressure-sensing devices and radar cannot duplicate the powers that Hemingway off-handedly—and unconvincingly—gives to Santiago. According to the Chief District Meteorologist of the United States Weather Bureau in Miami, Florida, Gordon E. Dunn, "It is usually impossible to see signs of a tropical storm for more than two days in advance and on occasion it is difficult to tell for sure that there is a tropical storm in the vicinity for even a day in advance."

Santiago as Fake

But it is when Santiago's fish makes its first appearance that the fakery truly begins to flow. For example, the old man perceives at once that it is a male. Hemingway heroes almost always measure themselves against male animals, whether they are kudu, lions, bear, bulls, or fish. The tragedy enacted in the bull ring becomes a farce if you replace the bull with a cow. The hunter, the torero, the fisherman prove that *they* have *cojones* by engaging another creature that has them

beyond dispute. Santiago's marlin is both huge and possessed of incredible endurance. He tows man and boat for
nearly three days.

But the marlin presents problems. Its *cojones* are internal.
"The sexes are not recognizable in these animals except by internal dissection," according to Gilbert Voss, an ichthyologist
with the University of Miami Marine Laboratory. Confronted
by this dilemma—by the need to pit his hero against a male
fish on the one hand, but a fish whose sex he won't be able to
determine by dissection before the sharks devour all the evidence, on the other—Hemingway resorts to the fakery of having Santiago identify him at once as a male. In an effort, perhaps, to make this bit of fakery more believable, Hemingway
has Santiago recall an experience with marlin in which he
was able to distinguish the male from the female.

> He remembered the time he had hooked one of a pair of mar-
> lin. The male fish always let the female fish feed first and the
> hooked fish, the female, made a wild, panic-stricken, de-
> spairing fight that soon exhausted her, and all the time the
> male had stayed with her, crossing the line and circling with
> her on the surface. He had stayed so close that the old man
> was afraid he would cut the line with his tail which was
> sharp as a scythe. . . . When the old man had gaffed her and
> clubbed her, . . . and then, . . . hoisted her aboard, the male
> fish had stayed by the side of the boat. Then while the old
> man was clearing the lines and preparing the harpoon, the
> male fish jumped high into the air beside the boat to see
> where the female was and then went down deep. . . . He was
> beautiful, the old man remembered, and he had stayed.

Santiago's story of the devoted male marlin actually
creates more problems than it solves. It is a preposterous
piece of natural history, combining sentimentality and inex-
act observation. The Associate Curator of Fishes of the
American Museum of Natural History, who was also a friend
of Hemingway's, Francesca LaMonte, noticed an interesting
parallel between Santiago's story and one Hemingway re-
counts in his marlin essay in *American Big Game Fishing:*

> Another time . . . my wife caught a 74-pound white marlin
> which was followed by three other marlin all through the fight.
> These three refused bait but stayed with the female fish until
> she was gaffed and brought aboard. Then they went down.

Miss LaMonte comments on this story that "You will note
that the sex of the other fishes is not stated." Hemingway has
Santiago incredibly enough identify the uncaught fish as
males but in his essay he is more realistic.

> ### No Emotion
>
> The trouble with *The Old Man* seems to be something else altogether, actually an opposite kind of trouble. Now the emotion is neither inferior nor maudlin: it simply seems to be missing. There is no lack of restraint or, at any rate, of the appearance of restraint. On the contrary, everything in the book gives the effect of having been pared down to the bone, and nothing comes through that is not carefully monitored and mediated and made to appear terribly *chosen*. But the difficulty is that one has no sense of what temptations were withstood, what incoherences and violences of feeling were brought under control, in order to achieve this effect. The whole vital Hemingway dimension of simplicity forced under enormous pressure out of complexity is absent from it.
>
> In the best of the early Hemingway it always seemed that if exactly the right words in exactly the right order were not chosen, something monstrous would occur, an unimaginably delicate internal warning system would be thrown out of adjustment, and some principle of personal and artistic integrity would be fatally compromised. But by the time he came to write *The Old Man* there seems to have been nothing at stake except the professional obligation to sound as much like Hemingway as possible. The man had disappeared behind the mannerism, the artist behind the artifice, and all that was left was a coldly flawless façade of words.
>
> John W. Aldridge, *Time to Murder and Create*, 1966.

Santiago and his fish are yoked by Hemingway's method of using the animal to epitomize some aspect of the man. The result, as Carlos Baker admiringly puts it, is "gallantry against gallantry." It is in fact more nearly fakery against fakery: a make-believe super-fish duelling a make-believe super-fisherman.

Some Realism

It must be conceded that leaving aside these two formidable adversaries, there are brilliant flashes of Hemingway realism in *The Old Man and the Sea*. The sharks, for example, are depicted with remarkable vividness as they rush the dead marlin and savagely tear it apart. The shovel-nosed sharks with their "wide, flattened, shovel-pointed heads . . . and their slitted yellow cat-like eyes" are made "good and true enough" so that they are convincing as sharks *and* as embodiments of pure evil.

With the mako shark, however, Hemingway has not wholly resisted the impulse to fake. He has claimed for the mako that he can swim "as fast as the fastest fish in the sea" and equipped him with eight rows of teeth "shaped like a man's fingers when they are crisped like claws. They were nearly as long as . . . fingers . . . and they had razor-sharp cutting edges on both sides." E.M. Schroeder, of the Harvard Museum of Comparative Zoology, an authority on the sharks of the Atlantic, and other shark experts seriously doubt that the mako is as fast as the fastest fish. And they find support from Hemingway who in an article in *Game Fish of the World* says that the mako can "run faster than most," and in another article mentions the tuna and wahoo as "the fastest fish in the sea."

To describe the mako as having eight rows of teeth, as Hemingway does, is a great deal like saying that a five-year-old child has forty or so teeth. Only two rows of the shark's teeth are functional; the others are replacements which become functional as the forward teeth are lost or destroyed. Also, according to Professor Voss, only the main teeth in the mid part of the shark's jaw are as long, slender, and sharp as Hemingway describes *all* the teeth as being. Just as Santiago and his fish are given extraordinary powers they could not in fact possess, the biggest and most dangerous of the sharks, the mako, is made more menacing than he actually is.

AN ASSUMPTION OF REALISM

Why are these inaccuracies of any consequence? No one thinks less of Keats's sonnet "On First Looking into Chapman's Homer" because in it Keats confused "stout Cortez" with Balboa as the discoverer of the Pacific; nor have the numerous anachronisms in Shakespeare's plays diminished his reputation or our enjoyment of his plays. Don't we read imaginative literature with an entirely different attitude toward fact from the one with which we consult an encyclopedia? The answer must be yes, but a qualified yes. We do not read either Keats or Shakespeare with the same expectations or assumptions as those we have when we read Hemingway. Hemingway is above all a realist; his aim had always been to communicate the facts exactly; and his reputation rests squarely on his success in doing so. As we read a Hemingway story or novel, his preoccupation with factual detail is immediately apparent. It is nowhere more apparent than in his heroes' respect for accuracy and a firm grip on the facts. Frederic Henry speaks for Hemingway, too, in what is probably the best known passage in *A Farewell to Arms* when he says: "Abstract words such as glory, honor, courage, or hallow were obscene beside the concrete names of villages, the number of roads, the names of rivers, the numbers of regiments and the dates." In short, the facts. And, likewise, those characters whom Hemingway places in contrast to his heroes are most readily distinguished not by their lack of honor, their insensitivity, or their political allegiances but by their sloppy handling of the facts. There is no clearer example of this than the tourist couple at the end of *The Old Man and the Sea* who look down into the water from the Terrace, see the skeleton of Santiago's great marlin, and ignorantly mistake it for a shark.

And Hemingway saw himself as a realist, too. His task in *The Old Man and the Sea,* as he saw it, was to give us a *real* old man, a *real* fish, and a *real* sea that would, if he had made them truly and well, mean many things. This is a reasonable definition of the goal of any realistic writer and provides us with a useful gauge of Hemingway's achievement. However, many critics have turned Hemingway's gauge upside down and upon discovering that the story of the old Cuban fisherman's ordeal can mean many things have praised it without troubling themselves to discover if the old man, the fish, and the sea are indeed "real," if they are indeed made "good and true."

The realism of Hemingway's first published stories is not an arbitrarily selected technique: it is an inevitable part of his world view. Confronted by the violence and meaninglessness of the world he saw as a boy in upper Michigan, as an 18-year-old police reporter on the *Kansas City Star,* and as a young man on the Italian front in World War I, in the Greco-Turkish War, and in the cities of Europe in the 1920's, he cultivated a bare, stoical, tight-lipped style that was an ideal instrument for exploring that God-abandoned world. The bullfighters, expatriates, soldiers, boxers, and guerillas were rendered vividly but truly and objectively. And their stance, if they were among the initiated, was much like the style that depicted them, one of tense control, like Nick Adams' trout holding itself steady against the current of the Big Two-Hearted River.

Too Chummy

But the style has gone soft in *The Old Man and the Sea* because the view of the world has gone soft. Santiago's universe is not the chaotic universe in which Nick Adams, Frederic Henry, Jake Barnes, and Robert Jordan encountered meaningless violence and evil. It is more nearly a cozy universe in which fish have nobility and loyalty and other virtues no one since St. Francis of Assisi—and least of all Ernest Hemingway—would have suspected them of. It is a universe so chummy that the hero calls various birds his brothers. The sharks introduce a semblance of evil into this warm universe, but it tends to be a stagey, melodramatic evil almost too villainous to be believable. The same is true of the big Portuguese man-of-war trailing its poisonous tentacles as it sails by Santiago's skiff fully six months before an animal this size would normally appear in Cuban waters.

The soft, fuzzy tone of *The Old Man and the Sea* reaches its nadir in that scene shortly after sunset when the incredible old man, still being towed by his incredible fish, looks into the heavens and sees the first star of this universe shining out. Hemingway comments: "He did not know the name of Rigel but he saw it and knew soon they would all be out and he would have all his distant friends." This cosmic camaraderie is patently false and forced. This is not the violent, chaotic world that young Hemingway discovered and explored with a style whittled from a walnut stick. In that world the stars were cold and remote—as stars really are. In the world of *The Old Man and the Sea*, they are "friends" whom the author in a patronizing intrusion identifies for us—incorrectly. Rigel does not appear in Cuban skies at sunset in September but some five hours after Santiago sees it. It is, perhaps, a trifling error, which, even if we happen to be aware of it, does not surprise us in a novel in which so much else is inexactly observed or tricked out in an effort to extort more feeling than a reasonable person would find there.

The honest, disciplined quest for "the way it was" finally ran down. *The Old Man and the Sea* stands as an end point of that quest. Yet it is not without greatness. To call it an inferior Hemingway novel still leaves it standing well above most other novels of our time. But some of its greatness is that of a monument serving to remind us of earlier glories.

CHAPTER 3

The Character of the Old Man

READINGS ON
THE OLD MAN AND THE SEA

The Old Man Maintains a Fighting Code

Wolfgang Wittkowski

In the following selection, professor Wolfgang Wittkowski contends that *The Old Man and the Sea* reiterates the theme of many of Hemingway's novels:
that of the ethical fighter. Wittkowski discounts critical interpretations that claim the book is religious in
nature, instead advocating that the Christian themes
are meant as allusions comparing the old man's
fight to that of Christ's. Wittkowski is professor
emeritus of German in the Department of Germanic
Languages and Literatures at the State University of
New York in Albany.

When *The Old Man and the Sea* appeared in 1952, Philip
Young wrote that it was a metaphor for life as a fight and
man as a fighter. It was a metaphor for which Hemingway
indicated his deep respect and enlists ours through the en-
hancing use of Christian symbols. That was the impression
of most readers then and probably is still today. However, in
1956 Carlos Baker gave a new twist to the critical discussion
of the story, one which had far-reaching consequences. He
stated that the religious associations attest to a Christian
mentality which in the course of the story's development
supplants the fighter ethos of the old man. This encouraged
several critics to point out Santiago's insight into the tragic
limitations of humanity and the consequent victory for a
democratic and interpersonal way of thinking. . . .

Let us look somewhat more closely at the rhetoric, the
paradoxical hyperbole, attending this attitude. It occurs
whenever Santiago considers the seriousness of his situation.
When he cannot open his cramped left hand he avers: "If I
have to have it, I will open it, cost whatever it costs." He will
not admit his exhaustion and he even claims: "I feel good." On

three separate occasions he declares he will stay with the marlin "forever." And toward the end of the battle we read: "I must get him alongside, he thought. I am not good for many more turns. Yes you are, he told himself. You're good for ever." When he scarcely knows how he will continue the battle with the sharks he says: "I'll fight them until I die."

THE FIGHTER ETHIC

With the strong exaggerations of all these utterances Santiago attempts to bolster his confidence so severely put to the test. This is the "psyching" speech used by fighters in the ring, whose manner of metaphor is familiar to all readers of Hemingway. Santiago's "faith," "hope," and "confidence" are not to be equated with Christian faith and hope. Santiago's belong to the fighter-ethic, which has been stylized and intensified to the pathos of the demiurgic self-creator again and again in Santiago. Santiago evolves the meaning of his remembered victory in hand-wrestling solely for the purpose of "giving himself more confidence." Back then he had been called "The Champion," "Santiago El Campéon." The rematch he had won easily by breaking his opponent's "confidence" while gaining himself the demiurgic proud confidence "that he could beat anyone if he wanted to badly enough."

Confrontation and victory in competitive sport serve here as the model, the ideal, and ultimately the metaphor. The same holds true for the baseball games whose results Santiago studies carefully and sorely misses when out to sea. The superlative champion he simply calls "the great DiMaggio," just as Manolin, his partner in these dialogues, reverently says "Jota" instead of J. when speaking of "the great John J. McGraw." During the battle with the fish the thought of his idol is a source of inspiration, satisfaction, and even a sense of obligation for Santiago: "I must be worthy of the great DiMaggio." After his victory over the marlin, he remarks: "I think the great DiMaggio would be proud of me today." And when he has finally killed the Mako shark, he muses: "I wonder how the great DiMaggio would have liked the way I hit him on the brain?"

The fully conscious pride of the fighter and killer is unmistakable. Though it is also combined with humility and modesty, the seeming humility of comparing oneself with stronger persons and not with weaker ones does not destroy pride, but ennobles it. This humility, Santiago emphasizes, is "not disgraceful" and denotes "no loss of true pride." For him humility is not a primary virtue. It must adapt itself to pride, that is, subordinate itself to it.

On one occasion Manolin calls Santiago "the best fisherman," a title at first rejected by Santiago. That Jesus, too, was so named suffices for pushing Baker to construe the old man's modesty as Christian humility. That still does not work, however, for Manolin then repeats his assertion and this time Santiago accepts it: "Thank you. You make me happy." For all their humble intent, Santiago's subsequent reservations maintain this pride. He hopes that no fish will be strong enough to refute Manolin's opinion ("prove us wrong"), an opinion which he himself shares: "I may not be as strong as I think. . . . But I know many tricks and I have resolution." This he proves throughout the story.

CHRIST AS FIGHTER

Critics believe that along with "humility," the Christian virtue of "gentleness" could bridle pride. Santiago says to himself: "Rest gently now against the wood and think of nothing." Then "the old man rode gently with the small sea and the hurt of the cord across his back came to him easily and smoothly." One critic, Melvin Backman, believes that "suffering and gentle and wood blend magically into an image of Christ on the cross." Perhaps there exists here an "abstract relationship of words" of the kind that fascinated Hemingway, possibly even between "cross" and "across," just as surrounding this passage there are several specific allusions to Christ. At the same time these images commingle with the typical traits of the fighter. More appropriate to a fighter than to Christ is the admonition not to think, which occurs more often than the corresponding exhortation to think about only that which is encouraging. Shortly before this, the central concept of suffering finds its expression in the boxing notion of "taking it," an expression implying the willful acceptance of suffering: "he took his suffering." "Wood" and "comfortably" occur in close proximity. This is also the immediate meaning of "gentle" in the sentence cited. It calls to mind on the one hand Christ on the Cross, yet at the same time the fighter, too, who sits down, leans against the ropes and relaxes between rounds.

Such double associations of Christ and the fighter are encountered more and more frequently. Their meaning needs to be clarified. "Gentleness" in the Christian sense of suffering is, of course, never found in Santiago. His relationship with Manolin, the sea, and some animals could indeed be described as "gentle." But this does not justify the comparing of Santiago with Saint Francis, for Santiago only loves certain people and animals, while despising and detesting others. He also possesses "gentleness" as an adjunct to his cardinal virtue, that of a Spaniard's chivalrous pride. Several variations of this he manifests in his feeling of shame when pretending he has nets, a place to wash, and a meal; in his ability to receive gifts with honor; in his polite attentiveness toward his benefactor and companion during the meal; and in his chivalrous gesture of giving away the head and sword of the marlin to those who helped him a little though he himself had lost everything. Santiago is not "gentle" like Jesus, but rather like the fighters Ole Anderson, Robert Jordan and Richard Cantwell, who are called "gentle," but still do not feel as Christians do. The chivalrous character of his "gentleness" in particular calls to mind the wounded matador, who in spite of his "suffering" remains "gracious . . . completely calm and very gentle and courteous" toward the bystanders.

As in the case of "humility" it is wrong to interpret "gentle" in Christian terms simply because this word may be used in a Christian sense and because there are textual associations with Christ. In a non-Christian context these words could evoke a totally different and even diametrically opposed meaning, namely one of antithesis and secularization. After all, both words designate values that are completely of this world and, as ever, aligned with pride. It is through pride that Santiago's ethos clearly gains its unity and cohesion. It is its core. Referring to his pride Santiago repeatedly restores the unity and order of his will in the face of contrary inclinations. Therein lies the victory in his defeat. He is all the more able to gain this victory because those tendencies are integral to his fighter's code. That in turn is possible only because he applies this code to everything he does, and because, inversely, he views his every act as something to which the code is directly applicable, namely, a fight. Moreover, this fight is analogous to the combat of competitive sports and not to the battles of, say, work and everyday life.

To catch the marlin and defend it against the sharks is important for the fisherman. But risking his life to do so and continuing the battle when it has become purposeless and

even reckless, leading to a disintegration of physical being
("Something in my chest was broken") certainly does not
serve a man's livelihood but is solely the fulfillment of the
fighter's code. Santiago regards his profession as the arena
in which he wants to establish and maintain mastery in the
struggle for victory or defeat. Accordingly, he understands
his body not as the end result of his profession but as a mere
means. Like an athlete, he forces himself to eat and sleep, although he likes neither. In May he drinks the bad-tasting
shark liver oil and eats turtle eggs in order to be strong in the
fall for the large fish. He trains body and mind, controls
them, uses them with great economy, risking his body without reservation only if necessary. If his body does not satisfy
his demands, then he hates it and despises it. . . .

It was within the relationship of Santiago and the marlin
that critics thought they had uncovered a decisive transfor-
mation from pride to love and humility in Santiago, a cessa-
tion of the previous coexistence of pride and love, of the
greatest sin and the greatest virtue. Such was Baker's
thought, and he saw in it a "philosophical crux." But there is
no reason to do this. It is part of the ritual of the fighter that
opponents demonstrate good friendship at every opportunity. The matador, whose chief virtue according to Hemingway is pride, loves the bulls, precisely because he must kill
them. And in spite of the ofttimes deadly rivalry between
matadors they help each other in the arena, where the
"closest brotherhood there is" prevails.

Santiago addresses the fish as "brother":

> You are killing me, fish. But you have a right to. Never have I
> seen a greater or more beautiful, or a calmer or more noble
> thing than you, brother. Come on and kill me. I do not care
> who kills who.

The fighter's priorities, the validity of his code begins to
weaken. But victory here for the Christian values of love and
mercy would contradict what must follow. All emotions opposing the decision to kill are rejected. This is all the more possible as respect for one's opponent and ultimate union with
him are integral to the fighter's code. They confer nobility and
warmth upon the will to victory, and give it precedence. Thus
Santiago rejects as well every impulse of opposing emotions:

> Now you are getting confused in the head, he thought. You
> must keep your head clear. Keep your head clear and know
> how to suffer like a man. Or a fish, he thought.

Santiago calls the fish "brother" as an equal, ideal opponent and sharer in his destiny. Between them there exists the same lonely bond as between boxers in the ring or between matador and bull: "Now we are joined together. . . . And no one to help either of us." They are bound in a lonely way "beyond all the people of the world." Furthermore, what transpires between Santiago and his fish can be understood only by the few who, together with them, belong to what Hemingway loved to call the secret order of the initiated. The writer stresses the communion, the very kinship of these two in their combative and demiurgic mode of existence. This is what is meant when Santiago calls himself "a strange old man" and the marlin "old fish" and says of the marlin that it behaves "strangely." As an attribute "strange" is regularly accompanied and clearly circumscribed by words such as "strong," "powerful," and "endure." In one instance such words refer to the fish, another time to fish and fisherman. He marvels at how the marlin battles, and when he thinks that the fish "decides to stay another night," even though that scarcely seems possible, he concedes to the animal the demiurgic self-determination which characterizes the expression of his own will.

In such union and kinship with his opponent, it is no wonder that Santiago feels compassion for the fish between rounds and when the pride of his victory has faded, compassion remains. It is the experience of the matador with an especially good bull, and it is Santiago's also. However, this is not evidence of a change in attitude on his part. Nor is his battle against the sharks.

> I killed the shark that bit my fish. And he was the biggest dentuso that I have ever seen. I wonder how the great DiMaggio would have liked the way I hit him on the brain? . . . But you enjoyed killing the dentuso. "And I killed him well."

A FIGHTER AND KILLER

This is not a man filled with Christian charity, as Baker maintains, but one with the pride and self-esteem of the fighter and killer. Certainly, this pride is founded to some extent upon pity and pain for the marlin, and ennobled by it, yet: "When the fish had been hit it was as though he himself were hit." "The sharks did not hit him again." "I cannot keep him from hitting me." "Come on Galanos."

Beyond attesting to communication between fish and fisherman these sentences reveal that above and beyond the now dead marlin, is a struggle between the man and the sharks. Santiago himself sees it as such. It again becomes important for him to fulfill the code of the fighter, to demonstrate the axiom: "A man can be destroyed but not defeated." In this he identifies with his dead opponent. And speaks to him: "But we have killed many sharks, you and I, and ruined others. How many did you kill, old fish?" This is how his final thoughts and words to the fish must be interpreted. Beyond any and all Christian feelings he is bound to the fish in antagonism toward the sharks and in the pride of the fighter and the killer.

This ethos outlives all other feelings mentioned. In the end, it is not a question of the marlin or the sharks, but simply of the fact that the old man has been defeated. It is his last thought upon returning and his first one after his sleep of exhaustion: "They beat me. . . . They truly beat me." He adds: "We must get a good killing lance and always have it on board." Just as before, he will go far out on the ocean to fight and kill. . . .

SIN IS FOREIGN

Those who give the story a Christian and moral interpretation are thus correct that allegiance to the code of the fighter and a feeling of sin are mutually exclusive. But they overlook the fact that the concept of sin remains wholly foreign to Santiago and his code:

> Do not think about sin, he thought.There are enough problems now without sin. Also I have no understanding of it.
> I have no understanding of it and am not sure I believe in it. Do not think about sin. It is much too late for that and there are people who are paid to do it. Let them think about it.

This is frivolous and even cynical. Hemingway is extending to the clergy his often documented contempt for the "uninitiated" who comment on art, war, and battle as a matter of routine and profit. It is also an anti-Christian polemic when Hemingway gives the impression that Santiago busies himself with the question of sin more for the sake of amusement, as a substitute for a radio or some reading material. Santiago's non-committal and mildly comical relationship to God and the saints is similarly worth noting. To be sure, he asks for their help, but only because his operating principle is to leave no stone unturned and no means untried. He relies far more upon himself. The figures of his faith are relics of his religious inheritance, just as the pictures in his cabin are "relics of his wife"; "I am not religious," he says. But, when Santiago does want to involve himself more deeply in matters of consequence, the simple fisherman is dependent upon the traditional concept of sin:

> You loved him when he was alive and you loved him after. If you love him, it is not a sin to kill him Or is it more?
> "You think too much, old man," he said aloud.
> But you enjoyed killing the dentuso, he thought.

As with the iceberg, beneath the surface of these awkward sentences lies the mass of Hemingway's philosophy of killing. The explanation ends abruptly, of course, for nothing can be accomplished through the concept of sin. After all, one is dealing with the axiom that one kills the opponent one respects and loves with enjoyment and pride. Killing, Hemingway says, is a feeling we cannot share with anyone. This "moment of truth" deepens the isolation from one's fellow man and intensifies the communion with an opponent as noble as the marlin. It also intensifies the awareness of being alive to the extent of believing oneself immortal and akin to God because of that immortality—just as the matador is God-like because he exercises the divine privilege of "administering death.". . .

VICTORY AND DEFEAT

Thus it is not now and never was really a question of crime and punishment, but one of victory and defeat, of applying the fighter's model. This Santiago does, and he does it arbitrarily. The fight with the marlin is kept separate from the fight with the sharks. The defeat in the latter does not count. Santiago remains champion. For the battle with the sharks does not correspond directly to the model of sport confrontation. On the other hand, in the fight with the sharks, Santiago still adheres to the fighter's code and ethos. He thus fulfilled his ethos so completely as to bring about his defeat. Moreover he demonstrated the way in which this ethos can be applied to fighting the sharks as well as to catching the marlin, and thus, in principle, to all endeavor. He determines demiurgically that his own misfortune is to take place and be judged "on his own terms."

The "as if," the imaginative arbitrariness with which life is seen in terms of sport combat and the sport's code has been called "quixotic gesture, quixotic pride." Critics justifiably pointed to the Existentialists. Santiago and his author also create through their actions an unbridgeable gap between themselves and the masses ("beyond all people"). But in so doing they do not leave their proper place in the order of things, in fact they assume it. It is not the purpose of their actions to set themselves apart from all other people. They make their own choice simply to demonstrate their ability to do so; they do it because they attribute the highest possible value to their chosen ethos and style of existence and because in the case of success they are not isolated but rather united in the secret order of the initiated.

This tendency to reduce and stylize existence to this fighter-in-the-ring model is easy to recognize in Hemingway's own life. It may be at work in his preference for the short story, in his habit of first conceiving novels as short stories, then as a connected sequence of individual scenes; and equally so in his characters. Superficially they can be divided into fighters or sufferers, but they are actually two sides of the same coin. . . .

Within the narrow confines of their fictional world these heroes also withdraw into a small special sphere which they can easily maintain. Their situations and behavior more or less resemble those of the fighter in the ring, whether actually or only in their own perceptions of things. Both are the case with Santiago, and one sees what he gains from them. Santiago's fundamental feelings of "Geworfensein" (being cast out into existence) and "Dennoch" (nevertheless) are transcended by the pride of having been set upon his life's course by virtue of the fighter's code which he has himself chosen. While everyday life was complicated for him, here he knows what moves against him and what he must do. Whether he wins or loses, he knows his worth and his place among his competitors, and his place in history. This gives his existence meaning, certainty, and unity. He proceeds with that "complete and respectful concentration on his world which marks all great artists" both in and out of the ring. At the climax of the fight he acts with the controlled rage that drives the very greatest and best of fighters "to go way past the impossible." By visualizing himself as a prize fighter in competition, set apart from the masses in the shadows beyond the ropes, he gains distance from and control over himself and "heroics" and "drama" as fascinating stylistic components of his existence. . . .

To find despair in the story of Santiago one has to read it into the story. In his discussion of luck the old man remarks, "Luck is a thing that comes in many forms and who can recognize her?". . . . But there is no question that he does experience luck, which a life in nature and intensification of existence in moments of greatest exertion can afford. The closing configuration of images, in which the old man in the hut dreams about the lions while down below the beheaded skeleton of the fish floats amidst garbage and cadavers, points to disintegration and death. Santiago is headed toward this. But that holds nothing frightening for him. . . . He is without family and scarcely allows himself a minimum amount of sleep and nourishment. The sea, whose clear "unimpressed blue" is reflected in his cheerful, unvanquished eyes, becomes for him "the one single, lasting thing." Now and then he frees himself from it, just as he does from the fish and his battle with them—once again the phenomenon of intensification—and then: "the lions are the main thing that is left." He happily dreams of them playing on the golden banks "so white they hurt your eyes." They may symbolize something akin to the undestroyed dead leopard beneath the dazzlingly white summit of Mt. Kilimanjaro, which the natives call "House of God," namely deliverance from the transitoriness and impurity of earthly things. There too, the religious association sanctifies something entirely of this world, namely a measure of ethical essence attained in death, the last "moment of truth." This measure is very great in Santiago's case, and he continues to subject himself to the *purgatio* and *castigatio* of his ascetic way of life and his enervating battles. But by bringing the basic form of life and the valid answer to it (namely suffering and acting) to perfect realization in battle and in the demiurgic fighter's ethos, he demonstrates and attains outside of Christianity a perfection which Hemingway, with the pride of Lucifer, places alongside and in opposition to that of Christianity. Furthermore, the fighter's ideal encompasses that which is truly authentic in Christ. It lays claim to the respect and esteem usually rendered to Christianity and its creator.

The Old Man Is a Spiritual Figure

William J. Handy

William J. Handy was an English professor at the University of Texas in Austin at the time he wrote the following selection. In it, Handy argues that Hemingway depicts the old man as spiritually fulfilled, even before he goes out to catch the marlin. Handy contends that throughout the novel's five distinct sections, the old man's spirituality grows as he eschews the practical and materialistic for a more enlightened stance.

Hemingway is not a naturalistic writer; he presents two worlds: On the one hand he envisions an internal world of singularly human values where the chief concern is with the being of the individual. On the other, he recognizes the external world of naturalistic values where the central focus is on the hopeless plight of man caught in the mechanism of a malevolent universe. Thus Hemingway's question is: What is to be the role of the individual man in a world which acts at every turn to determine his destiny? This is the basic problem throughout Hemingway's fiction. It is the problem confronting the young Hemingway hero Nick Adams in 'The Killers.' His answer is characteristic of a pattern Hemingway was to follow in nearly every work prior to *The Old Man and the Sea*: to detach himself from an environment whose value conditions he could not accept.

But what is perhaps most significant in Hemingway's various treatments of the problem of individual values is the fact that maintaining one's integrity is not so much a choice as it is a necessity. In 'The Snows of Kilimanjaro' he creates the pathetic image of a man who had compromised his sense of integrity. The story portrays the bitterness of a writer who was forced by his compromise to live a lie. Confronted with the fact of his rapidly approaching death, he

Excerpted from "A New Dimension for a Hero: Santiago of *The Old Man and the Sea*," by William J. Handy, in *Contemporary Novels: Six Essays in Modern Fiction*, edited by William O.S. Sutherland (Austin: Humanities Research Center, University of Texas). Copyright © 1962 by The University of Texas. Reprinted with permission.

remembers 'all the things he had wanted to write about,' and he realizes that it was precisely because his life had been a lie that he was now creatively impotent. . . .

THE OLD MAN HAS NO CONFLICT OF VALUES

In the portrayal of Santiago in *The Old Man and the Sea* there is no such uncertainty of being, no confusion of self and values. The old man is presented from beginning to end as one who has achieved true existence. His response to every situation is the response of a spiritually fulfilled man. The story, then, is not concerned with the familiar Hemingway search for values; rather it is concerned with the depiction of conflicting values.

Throughout five carefully delineated sections of the novel, the center of focus is always on the image of the old man. The first section concerns the old man and the boy; the second, the old man and the sea; the third, the old man and the marlin; the fourth, the old man and the sharks; the fifth section returns to the old man and the boy.

In the opening section Santiago is shown to be something of a pathetic figure. He is old, alone, except for the friendship of a young boy, and now even dependent to a degree upon the charity of others for his subsistence. His situation is symbolized by the condition of his sail which was 'patched with flour sacks and, furled, it looked like the flag of permanent defeat.' For eighty-four days he had fished without success and had lost his apprentice because the boy's parents had considered him 'salao,' 'the worst form of unlucky.'

But almost at once the tone of the writing changes. Only in external appearances is the old man pathetic. Hemingway reverses the attitude toward the old man in a single stroke:

> Everything about him was old except his eyes and they were the same color as the sea and were cheerful and undefeated.

The contrast in meaning is evident: To be defeated in the business of fishing is not to be a defeated man. The theme begins and ends the novel; never, after the opening lines does the reader regard Santiago as defeated. The point is made emphatic in the final conversation between the old man and the boy:

> 'They beat me, Manolin,' he said. 'They truly beat me.'
> 'He didn't beat you. Not the fish.'

And the old man, whose thoughts have been on a much more profound level of contesting, replies,

'No. Truly. It was afterwards.'

The novel's concern, then, is with success and failure, more precisely, with kinds of success and kinds of failure. The central contrast is between the two fundamental levels of achievement: practical success and success in the achievement of one's own being. Similarly the novel posits two kinds of defeat: Failure to compete successfully in a materialistic, opportunistic world where this only is the measure of a man and failure to maintain one's being regardless of external defeat. Thus the real story concerns the meaning, in terms of fundamental human values, of human existence.

Almost at once we become aware that the misleading initial depiction of the old man as a somewhat pathetic figure is the direct result of viewing him only from the standpoint of his recent prolonged ill luck. Had Hemingway continued to present Santiago through the eyes that measure a man's worth merely in terms of his practical success or failure, the novel would necessarily have been a naturalistic one. Santiago's skill, determination, and nobility of spirit would simply have contributed to the greater irony of his finally catching a prize fish only to worsen his lot by losing it.

But the key to all of Hemingway's major characters is never to be found . . . in merely what happens to them. Rather it is to be found in what they essentially are. This is not to discount the importance in Hemingway of environmental forces, both man-made and cosmic, acting to condition and even to determine human destiny. In fact, those whose values do not follow from the shaping forces of environment are few in number, rarely to be encountered. Santiago is one not determined by environment. And in his age and wisdom and simplicity he constantly reminds himself and the boy, who is learning from him, of the distinction. It is a subtle but vital distinction, one which Santiago never loses sight of. When the boy complains to Santiago about the attitude of his new master, Santiago's response is central to the underlying theme of the novel. The boy points out:

'He brings our gear himself. He never wants anyone to carry anything.'
'We're different,' the old man said.

The real story of *The Old Man and the Sea* begins with this distinction. In the first section two indistinct characters are introduced who embody the values of the practical world, the boy's father and the successful fisherman to whom the boy is assigned. In the old man and the boy's discussion of their enforced separation, we see the old man's simple recognition of the problem.

> 'Santiago,' the boy said to him as they climbed the bank from where the skiff was hauled up. 'I could go with you again. We've made some money.'
>
> The old man had taught the boy to fish and the boy loved him.
>
> 'No,' the old man said. 'You're with a lucky boat. Stay with them.'
>
> 'But remember how you went eighty-seven days without fish and then we caught big ones every day for three weeks.'
>
> 'I remember,' the old man said. 'I know you did not leave me because you doubted.'
>
> 'It was papa made me leave. I am a boy and I must obey him.'
>
> 'I know,' the old man said. 'It is quite normal.'

But the old man's response means something more than that it is quite normal for a boy to obey his parents; it means the acknowledgment that materialism is the central criterion for action and values in the practical world. And the passage also suggests that the boy has been taught something more than how to fish; he has been taught love and respect, values which he now finds conflicting with the practical demands of his parents.

The successful fisherman, the unnamed "he" who is the boy's new master, is, in spite of his success at catching fish, totally without respect in the boy's eyes. When Santiago promises to awaken the boy in time for his day's work with his new master, the boy declares,

> 'I do not like for him to waken me. It is as though I were inferior.'

The missing quality in the boy's new relationship is evident: The old man wakens the boy in order to share living with him; the impersonal 'him' wakes the boy in order to use him. . . .

There is no condemnation by the old man of those who do not share his values. He simply thinks of them as lacking wisdom, of being young or inexperienced:

> . . . many of the fishermen made fun of the old man and he was not angry. Others, of the older fishermen, looked at him and were sad. But they did not show it and they spoke politely about the current and the depths they had drifted their lines at and the steady good weather and of what they had seen.

PRACTICAL SUCCESS IRRELEVANT

For the 'older fishermen,' the 'those who belong' of the earlier novels, a man's worth is not dependent upon his practical success. Ill luck may contribute to or even bring about one's failure in the world of practical values, but it cannot change what he essentially is within himself. Thus, for the initiate, respect and recognition are not contingent upon chance; they are the acknowledgment of the achievement of true existence. And it is a central maxim in Hemingway's concept of man that one's inner being must be constant regardless of the chance happenings of an external world.

The novel's second section presents the full significance of what it means to possess the sense of true existence. Just as the 'he' who wakes the boy to use him is blocked by his practical ends from the experience of love so also the 'younger fishermen' whose intention is to exploit are prevented from regarding the sea as anything more than 'a contestant or a place or even an enemy.' Again the distinction is one of individual values:

> He always thought of the sea as *la mar* which is what people call her in Spanish when they love her. Sometimes those who love her say bad things of her but they are always said as though she were a woman. Some of the younger fishermen, those who used buoys as floats for their lines and had motorboats, bought when the shark livers had brought much money, spoke of her as *el mar* which is masculine. They spoke of her as a contestant or a place or even an enemy. But the old man always thought of her as feminine and as something that gave or withheld great favours, and if she did wild or wicked things it was because she could not help them.
>
> The moon affects her as it does a woman, he thought.

The passage is an important one in the development of the novel. Hemingway's theme is clear: Success in the achievement of being carries with it the most valued of man's possessions, the capacity for love. And Santiago's capacity is everywhere evident. Once far out in the Gulf the old man takes his place as a true inhabitant of his true environment. . . .

Santiago's struggle with the marlin is the principal subject of the long third section. From the moment he feels the fish touch the bait, his feeling is one of joy for the anticipated contest:

> Then he felt the gentle touch on the line and he was happy.
> 'It was only his turn,' he said. 'He'll take it.'
> He was happy feeling the gentle pulling and then he felt something hard and unbelievably heavy.

Throughout the long contest his attitude toward the fish remains constant:

> 'Fish,' he said. 'I love you and respect you very much. But I will kill you dead before this day ends.'
> Let us hope so, he thought.

A SUCCESSFUL QUEST

In *The Old Man and the Sea* Hemingway presents his hero in his finest hour. Santiago is a complete man who possesses courage, devotion, confidence, and purpose. . . . Santiago fully realizes his place in his world, and he refuses to break the rules and exploit nature or man. Man's dignity as a human being and his brotherhood with the natural world give Santiago meaning and satisfaction in living. Santiago, moreover, believes in a supreme being who gives him aid and comfort. Instead of becoming bitter when he recognizes his own limitations, Santiago seeks aid from God and finds comfort in being a part of the natural world. In Santiago, the Hemingway hero successfully completes what has been a long difficult quest for faith.

Gary D. Elliott, *McNeese Review*, vol. 24.

The events of the struggle are dramatic: From the time fish is hooked, about noon of the first day, until the fish is killed, about noon of the third day, the old man is forced to place his own body between the fish and boat. Fastening the line to the boat would result in the breaking of the line by any sudden lurch or swift motion by the fish. Thus the contest means for Santiago the summoning of his greatest efforts in skill and endurance. He carefully plans his strategy: Constant maximum pressure on the line must be maintained in order to wear down the resistance of the fish and to encourage him to surface in an attempt to dislodge the hook. Santiago knew that once having surfaced, the fish would be unable to dive deep again. Nourishment and rest must be systematically apportioned to his body so that he would not lose the battle prematurely through physical exhaustion. All effort must point to the final struggle which would involve not merely skill and physical endurance but will, his own will in mortal contest with the will of the marlin.

A CHANGING IMAGE

But the real power of the novel's impact does not lie merely in the events of the old man's dramatic struggle. It lies, I believe, in Hemingway's successful creation of a new dimension in dramatic portraiture. In each of the five carefully delineated sections of the novel, the reader's attention is always on Santiago. But in each, Hemingway alters with subtle but masterful strokes his changing image of the old man. In each he modifies the dramatic focus to isolate, intensify, and thereby magnify the novel's central and controlling image, the portrait of Santiago.

In the setting of the simple fishing village we are presented with the aged fisherman, initially pathetic in his meager existence, but admirable in his determination to break his run of bad luck, at once lovable in his touching relationship with a young boy and quaint in his concern for American baseball. But as a solitary figure on the sea, against a backdrop of cosmic nature, the image of the old man takes on new and greater proportions. He becomes a being among the beings of the sea, a human force among the forces of the natural world. But it is at the point at which the old man engages the great marlin that a more profound level of meaning is reached. Hemingway marks the shift with characteristic restraint. The change is simple but unmistakable:

> The boat began to move slowly off toward the North West.

It is here, I think, that the reader becomes aware that he is experiencing the achievement in prose which Hemingway had tried vaguely to explain in *Green Hills of Africa*. He had referred there to 'a fourth and fifth dimension that can be gotten.' And in speaking of the complexity of such writing, he had declared, 'Too many factors must combine to make it possible.' He had called such prose 'much more difficult than poetry,' but 'one that can be written, without tricks and without cheating. With nothing that will go bad afterwards.' In the amazing combination of simple realism of narrative and complex symbolism of image at once contained in *The Old Man and the Sea*, Hemingway has, I believe, constructed his closest approximation to his goal. . . .

Presented through the sensibility of the old man, the realistic event becomes transformed into a new subject matter—one which maintains the realism of the action, but which uses that action to objectify essentially human values and human responses. Santiago, the fisherman, participates in action, the action required for his practical livelihood, but Santiago, the man, also participates in existence, and human existence as he has achieved it is not confined by the limitations of a mere vital existence. The choice of the fish, however native to its instinct, had been to live beyond the snares and traps and treacheries of those who would destroy him. There is a note of compassion and regret in the old man's declaration: 'My choice was to go there to find him beyond all people. Beyond all people in the world.' The response is a contradiction to Santiago's earlier feeling of happiness, of 'joy for the anticipated contest.' Yet the very ambivalence expresses at once something of the paradox of the human situation.

Even the simple sentiments of love and benevolence which Santiago feels for the small creatures of the sea become more profoundly valid when they are presented through the larger awareness of the old man. He knows that the sea which he loves can also be cruel, and his ambivalent attitude toward the sea intensifies the presentation of the paradox:

> He was very fond of flying fish as they were his principal friends on the ocean. He was sorry for the birds, especially the small delicate dark terns that were always flying and looking and almost never finding and he thought, 'The birds have a harder life than we do except for the robber birds and the heavy strong ones. Why did they make birds so delicate and fine as those sea swallows when the ocean can be so cruel? She is kind and very beautiful. But she can be so cruel and it comes so suddenly and such birds that fly, dipping and hunting, with their small sad voices are made too delicately for the sea.'

The passage contains an implicit lament. The old man's question is reminiscent of Ahab's unhappy speculation on the forces of malice in the universe. Yet there is no defiance or anger directed to the impersonal 'they' who have made a universe which permits the simultaneous existence of good and evil, of helplessness and gentleness amid destructive forces. Rather in the old man's reflections there is sympathy and compassion of an awareness capable of comprehending the paradoxical mystery of the struggle for existence. . . .

Hemingway's subject matter never involves a mere external conflict; in all of the major short stories and the novels, it involves also an internal conflict, a struggle on the level of being. Santiago's being is much more complex than that of the pathetic figure in the anecdote. The complexity of his sensibility and his values is most evident in his ability to transcend the vital or subsistence level of his experience. And his reflections bring together symbolically the two levels of value which comprise the universal problem of all men, the necessity to destroy what at the same time one loves:

> Then he was sorry for the great fish that had nothing to eat and his determination to kill him never relaxed in his sorrow for him. How many people will he feed, he thought. But are they worthy to eat him? No, of course not. There is no one

worthy of eating him from the manner of his behavior and his
great dignity. I do not understand these things, he thought.
But it is good that we do not have to try to kill the sun or the
moon or the stars. It is enough to live on the sea and kill our
true brothers.

It is in his values that Santiago has gone 'far out'; it is in
his values that he is 'a strange old man.' His questions and
speculations would have no relevance for the old fisherman
of the anecdote because for him they would simply not exist.
The profound difference between what the two fishermen
would hold as important is most evident at the point at
which Santiago's battle with the fish is won. His victory is a
complex one, and, for Hemingway, the complexity defines
what an actualized man can be:

> I want to see him he thought, and to touch and to feel him. He
> is my fortune, he thought. But that is not why I wish to feel
> him. I think I felt his heart, he thought. When I pushed on the
> harpoon shaft the second time.

In the fourth section, the battle with the sharks, going 'far
out' with all its ramifications for man's existence on the level
of being, becomes going 'out too far.' A new kind of struggle
begins with the simple statement.

> It was an hour before the first shark hit him,

which contains the full sense of the inevitability of those
forces which the old man engaged when he had extended
the limits and security of the practical world. Hemingway
follows the statement with another possessing the same
force achieved by his characteristic restraint, saying at once
more than could have been said by any other technique:

> The shark was not an accident.

Now, on the level of being, begins much more than a struggle to retain his prize of fifteen hundred pounds which would
'dress out two thirds of that at thirty cents a pound.' The struggle with the sharks is a struggle of hate, the counterpart to the
struggle of love which had characterized his encounter with the
fish. When Santiago drives the harpoon at the oncoming shark,
Hemingway formulates the essential difference: 'He hit it without hope but with resolution and complete malignancy.' And
when some forty pounds of the marlin had been torn away, the
loss is something different in kind of value from market loss:

> He did not like to look at the fish anymore since it had been
> mutilated. When the fish had been hit it was as though he
> himself were hit.

Again all levels of subject matter and technique come together when the greater-than-life image of the old man is abruptly brought in contact with the first of the two 'hateful' Galanos sharks, those which are 'scavengers as well as killers.'

> 'Ay,' he said aloud. There is no translation for this word and perhaps it is just such a noise such as a man might make, involuntarily, feeling the nail go through his hands and into the wood.

The allusion is daring. Its function is to suggest the degree of the pain of recognition when a man with Santiago's capacity for love is confronted with the naked being of malevolence. Hemingway leaves no doubt about the essential nature of these objectifications of malevolence.

> It was these sharks that would cut the turtle's legs and flippers off when the turtles were asleep on the surface, and they would hit a man in the water, if they were hungry, even if the man had no smell of fish blood nor of fish slime on him.

Santiago's response is once again a response of being:

> 'Ay,' the old man said. '*Galanos.* Come on *Galanos.*'

In the long struggle to follow the old man loses the battle to save his fish. But the far more important battle, that which pits the being of the old man against the being of nature's malevolent forces, is not lost. This is the theme of the section. It is stated simply and directly in Santiago's utterance to the sea:

> . . . man is not made for defeat. . . .'
> 'A man can be destroyed but not defeated.'

In the final short section, the focus shifts to the boy, Manolin. The initial problem, how the boy would once again accompany the old man, is not solved on the practical level of the success or failure of Santiago's venture 'far out.' Its solution takes place within the being of the boy after the full realization of the old man's experience registers itself upon the boy's sensibility:

> He was asleep when the boy looked in the door in the morning. It was blowing so hard that the drifting-boats would not be going out and the boy had slept late and then come to the old man's shack as he had come each morning. The boy saw that the old man was breathing and then he saw the old man's hands and he started to cry. He went out very quietly to go to bring some coffee and all the way down the road he was crying.
> Many fishermen were around the skiff looking at what was lashed beside it and one was in the water, his trousers rolled up, measuring the skeleton with a length of line.

The boy did not go down. He had been there before and one of the fishermen was looking after the skiff for him.

'How is he?' one of the fishermen shouted.

'Sleeping,' the boy called. He did not care that they saw him crying. 'Let no one disturb him.'

Thus even though he has failed to bring his fish to market, Santiago's feat has touched a responsive chord in the fishermen of the village. He is once more *El Campeón*. But it is within the boy, because of his deep caring for the old man, that the most significant response occurs. It is a response that resolves the initial problem, at once removing the problem from the level of practical success and placing it on the level of the achievement of being:

'Now we fish together again.'

'No, I am not lucky. I am not lucky anymore.'

'The hell with luck,' the boy said. 'I'll bring the luck with me.'

The boy's decision recalls a similar decision made by a boy in what Hemingway has called the greatest American novel, *Huckleberry Finn*. There Huck, forced to choose between the demands of a conscience which had been conditioned by the conventions and mores of society to turn over the runaway slave, Jim, and the demands of his own love for Jim as an individual being, declares: 'All right, then, I'll go to hell,' and makes his decision on the side of being. Like Huck's, Manolin's decision is a recognition of the clashing values of a practical world and the world of individual values. His decision represents the point of his maturity.

In the brief closing scene, the focus is withdrawn in a way that places the drama of conflicting values which defined Santiago's struggle back in the larger context of man's existence in civilized society. For the woman and her companion who belong to the party of tourists who are 'at the Terrace looking down in the water among the empty beer cans and dead barracudas,' there is no awareness of the kind of drama which is symbolized by the skeleton of the great marlin 'that was now just garbage waiting to go out with the tide.' They suggest those whose existence is comfortably detached, those who will never 'go far out,' those for whom the problem of man's being and man's fundamental values is no problem.

The Old Man's Classic Quest

Robert O. Stephens

Robert O. Stephens was assistant professor of English at the Women's College of the University of North Carolina. He has published articles on Hemingway and on Texas oil history. In this selection, Stephens contends that the old man transcends his animal nature in *The Old Man and the Sea* to achieve a spiritual enlightenment. The old man's exhaustion at the end of the book, Stephens concludes, is meant to point out that such enlightenment is not achieved without suffering and, ultimately, death.

When Ernest Hemingway told George Plimpton of the *Paris Review* about his iceberg theory of writing, he pointed to *The Old Man and the Sea* as a prime example of such writing. According to the theory, "I always try to write on the principle of the iceberg. There is seven-eighths of it under water for every part that shows." The sea novel in respect to style fits the theory, Hemingway pointed out, in that he knew many fishing stories never explicitly incorporated in the tale; knowing them gave him authority for the tale he did write. But Hemingway suggested more strongly the applicability of the iceberg image for understanding theme when he noted, "You can be sure that there is much more than will be read at any first reading. . . ." This comment is especially meaningful when used as a way of viewing a theme in his work that emerges like the crest of an iceberg in this novel.

That theme is the vision of man as animal trying to transcend his animal nature. In *The Old Man and the Sea* this theme, latent in many early works and of secondary consideration in others, emerges as the true basis of the Hemingway protagonist's tragic view of life. The exact nature of that tragic view is, I think, impossible to determine until the sea

Excerpted from Robert O. Stephens, "Hemingway's Old Man and the Iceberg," *Modern Fiction Studies*, vol. 7, Winter 1961–1962, pp. 295, 298–304. Copyright 1961 by The Johns Hopkins University Press. Reprinted by permission of The Johns Hopkins University Press.

novel is seen as its explication. In recognizing the vital role of animal imagery in Hemingway's earlier works, we find that one of the chief beauties of *The Old Man and the Sea* is the clarity with which earlier animal images take meaning within the context of the sea novel. . . .

TRIUMPHING OVER THE ANIMAL

The culminative recognition Santiago makes is the triumph man has over his animal existence by his ability to understand his fate when he cannot avoid it biologically. To transcend his animal fate, he looks to what he has in addition to animal nature and finds that his moral nature opens the way to triumph. In exploiting his moral nature, Santiago finds a resolution as classically ancient as the Adamic myth: to understand the process is to escape the effect of the process.

Santiago's insight is parallel to that described by critic A.O. Lovejoy as the Paradox of the Fortunate Fall. Man rises above his animal state by usurping a godlike attribute: knowledge. Making a choice to gain knowledge, he both gains moral stature and dooms himself to death as the price of his usurpation. But even as he dooms himself to physical deterioration, he opens the way to spiritual enlightenment, which becomes a possibility because of his moral nature. Hemingway's conception of this relationship between man and animal is evident in *Death in the Afternoon.* Characterizing the matador, he writes that "when a man is still in rebellion against death he has pleasure in taking to himself one of the Godlike attributes: that of giving it. This is one of the most profound feelings in those who enjoy killing."

The Old Man and the Sea thus becomes the crest of the metaphorical iceberg; the animal theme is brought into the open, and we can see the direction in which the theme has been developing in the earlier works.

If the paradox at the heart of the sea novel is similar to that at the core of the Adamic myth, Hemingway nevertheless presents it in terms commensurate with his protagonists of the twentieth century. In terms the protagonist accepts as valid, the paradox concerns the problem of how to win by losing, or of how to remain champion by being defeated. Critics since the time of "The Undefeated" have seen the protagonists achieve a triumph in defeat through stoic virtues of endurance. But what *The Old Man and the Sea* reveals is that the paradoxical triumph comes about through the protagonist's recognition of his moral nature. This is the idea that gives order to the narrative details of the novel.

THE SYMBOLIC SEA

Understanding Hemingway's use of the sea as setting and symbol is necessary for perceiving the operation of the paradox, for the sea is the general instrument of defeat for the hero. . . . Santiago is withdrawn not only from society and civilization but also from the rest of humanity. He faces the sea as an amoral universe, a capricious woman, *la mar*, who gives favors but also cannot help doing cruel things. Within this framework of chaos exist the Portuguese man-of-war ("*Agua mala*. . . . You whore"), the loggerhead turtles which Santiago loves and which eat the Portuguese men-of-war, and the rapacious sharks which eat the loggerheads as well as eat men. He also sees the incipient tragedy of the small sea bird, standing in analogy to the spirit of man, as it battles the elements of the sea. Watching the bird compete with the dolphins for the flying fish, Santiago notes that the bird has no chance against the bigger and faster fish. And after he has hooked the marlin and a warbler comes to rest on the line, Santiago observes that it will soon learn it is the prey of hawks.

But the sharks are the dramatic instruments of the old man's defeat by the sea. They come not by accident but as natural results of spilling the marlin's blood. It is physical nature against physical nature as Santiago fights them with harpoon, knife, and tiller and the sharks rip the carcass. Only the head, tail, and skeleton of the marlin remain to record the great catch. What might have been a physical triumph has been taken back by natural process. That the marlin represents Santiago's physical nature during the melee is evident in his pain as the fish is mutilated. The loss of the marlin as a physical achievement suggests Santiago's sense of death as physical extinction. Fighting the last shark, he has the taste of copper in his mouth, and as he spits at the shark, he cries, "Eat that, *Galanos*. And make a dream you've killed a man." He reports the taste later to Manolin as an ominous sign: "In the night I spat something strange and felt something in my chest was broken." In this respect, then, he is in the empathic position of having known death and having come back to explain.

The defeat, however, is only a test of the values Santiago

derives in the contest with the marlin. His triumph over the marlin gives him poise and comprehension for enduring the work of the sharks. And his triumph, more importantly, is confirmed upon his return to shore with only the skeleton relic of his victory. What happens on the shore could not have happened had not the defeat by the sharks taken place on the sea.

THE ATTAINMENT OF VALUES

The paradoxical triumph has two parts: the derivation and recognition of spiritual values, on the one hand, and the confirmation of those values, on the other. The preliminary victory over the marlin begins when Santiago chooses to go beyond the "well" of traditional fishing grounds and on to the outer stream. Thus, early is introduced the theme of choice that runs throughout the conflict at sea. When he snares the great marlin, Santiago notes that it had been the choice of the fish to go far out and that now they are in conflict by choice: "His choice had been to stay in the deep dark water far out beyond all snares and traps and treacheries. My choice was to go there to find him beyond all people. Beyond all people in the world. Now we are joined together and have been since noon."

Attributing choice to the fish thus becomes acceptable when Santiago's identification of his animal nature with the fish becomes evident. At first the marlin is an unknown force; the old man knows only that he has hooked something and wishes to see what it is he is fighting. After he has seen the fish and has been awed by his great size, Santiago begins to establish the identification between himself and the beast: "Keep your head clear and know how to suffer like a man. Or a fish, he thought." And after his triumph over the marlin, when the sharks have begun to strike, he avoids looking at the mutilated beast because "When the fish had been hit it was as though he himself were hit." The connection between marlin and man becomes more evident in the semi-betrayal of Santiago's hand to the physical demands represented by the fish. The hand becomes animalistic as it becomes like a claw: "What kind of hand is that. . . . Cramp then if you want. Make yourself into a claw." He further notes the hand's betrayal as a treachery of one's body: diarrhea humiliates one before others, but the cramp humiliates him when he is alone. The identification becomes a step clearer when he observes, "There are three things that are brothers: the fish and my two hands." The kinship between hand and the rest of the natural process is established fully when the sharks come. The Mako shark's teeth are "shaped like a man's fingers when they are crisped like claws."

Yet if the hand is part of biological nature, the strength of the hand, like the strength of the marlin, is a measure of the man who overcomes the animal force. The hand finally becomes obedient to the mind of Santiago. That animal force over which the mind triumphs was measured once, for example, in the contest with the negro from Cienfuegos at the tavern in Casablanca. Santiago won the contest by his confidence in himself as a man and champion and triumphed over the brute strength of the negro, who lacked the champion's pride.

MEN FIGHTING BEASTS

His identification with the great fish puts Santiago in the classic line of men fighting beasts as symbols of their own internal struggles between human pride and animal instinct—the Cretans, for example, wrestling bulls as a religious rite. He is an extension of the Hemingway matadors as they dominate the instinctive destruction of the bulls in the tragic spectacle of the *corrida*. Indeed, Santiago is a matador of marlins and experiences the same pride and elation felt by the tauromaquian matadors as they, through skill and intelligence, assert their godlike power of dominating animal instinct and then demonstrate triumph over such instinct by killing it. The contest between man and fish progresses much as does a bullfight with its ordered sequence of action. Santiago is the member of the *cuadrilla* exploring the hooking habits of the bull as he strives to find what kind of fish he has on the line. He is the *picador* as he strikes with the line to set the hook safely in the marlin's mouth. As he lashes the two oars across the stern of the boat to increase the drag, he is the *banderillero* lacing the barbs to slow the bull. But as the matador, the dominator of the beast, he shows greatest skill and courage. He must keep an optimum pressure on the line to wear down the marlin without sending the fish out in a rush of strength to break the line; he is the matador balancing self-exposure against domination. Finally he sees the fish swing east with the current, a signal of surrender to the will of the handler. As the fish begins to circle, Santiago puts a strain on the line to shorten the circles and finally maneuvers the marlin alongside for the kill just as the matador positions the bull. And just as the matador drops the *muleta* for the fatal instant in order to make the sword thrust, Santiago drops the line to drive in the harpoon.

All the time he is demonstrating his mastery over the marlin Santiago realizes that he is able to do so because of his human intelligence. He asserts the Adamic pride of intellect over instinct: "He is a great fish and I must convince him. . . . I must never let him learn his strength nor what he could do if he makes his run. If I were him I would put in everything now and go until something broke. But, thank God, they are not as intelligent as we who kill them; although they are more noble and more able." As the fish circles the boat, Santiago realizes that he must "convince" the fish before killing him; and after he has harpooned the marlin, he knows "I am only better than him through trickery. . . ."

But this trickery is a special kind. It includes all the mental processes through which Santiago gains spiritual strength during the long contest. Even though his physical strength is less than that of the fish, his morale makes his strength more effective than his opponent's. His practical wish to have the boy Manolin as a helper, for example, becomes a wish for the strength he, Santiago, had in his more vigorous and confident days. He makes the boy into a memory image of himself. His memory of the young lions on the African beaches recalls his own youthful strength. The memory of his victory over the negro from Cienfuegos also reminds him of his claim to be *El Campeón*. And he derives strength from thinking of that other champion DiMaggio, who also won in spite of the bone spur in his heel.

CALLING ON GOD'S AID

Also part of this "trickery" is the secret ritual characteristic of the Hemingway hero. Here the ritual is the prayer for control of luck. It too is a form of self-explanation for the old man. When, earlier, he tells Manolin that he had rather have skill than luck, he hopes that conditions will remain within his power to control. But finally he recognizes, as do the other Hemingway perceivers of *nada*, that chaotic natural process will be too much for him. He resorts to the rituals to bring some small order, however arbitrary, into the chaos. Thus, when he can do nothing more to fashion the world his own way, Santiago calls on God to make the marlin strike hard at the bait, to make the fish jump, and to remove the cramp from his hand. The Our Fathers and Hail Marys only formalize this ritual tendency. That these rituals belong to the period of enlightenment is confirmed by their absence during the onslaught of the sharks. The rituals, like the memory images, are part of the moral illumination that gives Santiago power to transcend the physical degradation.

Thought, then, is the difference between man and beast. At first Santiago attempts only to endure, not think. But he realizes that he must think in order to do nothing false while working the marlin. His talking to himself then becomes a vocal sign of his thought process: "It encouraged him to talk because his back had stiffened in the night and it truly hurt now."

As his thoughts form, the old man begins to understand his relationship with the fish. True, the fish is an extension of his own bodily instincts, but his killing the fish is an act of proud contempt for his physical limitations. His thinking collides with the paradox of biological and intellectual forces within the same being. He recognizes the consequences of intellect as he muses over the marlin he has just killed: "You did not kill the fish only to keep alive and sell for food. . . . You killed him for pride and because you are a fisherman." The value of the preliminary contest with the marlin is that in the contest he has learned the implications of his moral nature. He has achieved understanding that survives biological destruction: "A man can be destroyed but not defeated." The basis of his undefeatability is his pride, which both subjects him to defeat because of his choice— "You violated your luck when you went too far outside"— and sends him out to attempt the impossible, to attempt more than he could achieve within the "well." His capacity for attempting too much is both self-defeating and ennobling. His pride is a mark of the godlike quality that transcends animal fate.

A GROWING ENLIGHTENMENT

The confirmation of this insight occurs in the Christ motif, which, appearing thinly at first in the novel and gradually becoming dominant, suggests the growing illumination of the protagonist. Santiago's drinking of the shark liver oil, in light of the sharks' role as messengers of death, takes on eucharistic overtones. When he sees the two *galano* sharks streaking toward the marlin, the old man cries, "*Ay,*" which is "just such a noise as a man might make, involuntarily, feeling the nail go through his hands and into the wood." Going up the hill after his return to shore, he carries the mast across his shoulders like a cross and stumbles on his way to the summit of the hill. On top of the hill, lying in his shack, he sleeps face down "with his arms out straight and the palms of his hands up," in the position of a man crucified. Like the Jew noted by the Roman soldier of "Today is Friday," Santiago was "pretty good in there today." He asserts by his example that there are human qualities for which death is not final. He completes the paradox that to win spiritually, one must lose biologically; to survive animal fate, one must suffer it.

All this is not to say that in his earlier works Hemingway perceives or accepts this paradoxical position. Rather, he makes irregular steps in this direction. In the earliest stories he demonstrates a consciousness of the biological trap. But in the books of the twenties and forties he seems to be looking for an escape from the trap by way of social values, whether of fugitive societies of expatriates or of the Spanish gypsy type. He seems most directly on the track of the moral discovery in *The Old Man and the Sea* when he is investigating the implications of bullfighting and hunting in the books of the thirties. The attempts of Harry of "Kilimanjaro" to find spiritual values in the face of biological decay most nearly approach the insight of Santiago.

But even in the sea novel Hemingway does not abandon social perpetuation of the protagonist's discovery. . . .

Santiago is to make his insight available to Manolin. Appropriately, the knowledge is perpetuated in terms of action rather than words, for it is in action that the knowledge is derived. Thus Manolin says at last, "But we will fish together now for I have much to learn," and, "You must get well fast for there is much that I can learn and you can teach me everything."

In Hemingway's tragic vision of man as animal, therefore, *The Old Man and the Sea* serves as the crest of the iceberg in several ways. But primarily it serves to explain that vision in open, if symbolic, terms.

The Old Man's Heroic Struggle

Leo Gurko

Well-known literary critic Leo Gurko was professor of English at Hunter College and the author of numerous works, including *The Angry Decade: Heroes, Highbrows, and the Popular Mind* and *The Two Lives of Joseph Conrad*. In this selection, Gurko argues that the old man, more than any other character in Hemingway's novels, is a hero because, among other things, he "has not been permanently wounded or disillusioned."

Most of Hemingway's novels emphasize what men cannot do, and define the world's limitations, cruelties, or built-in evil. *The Old Man and the Sea* is remarkable for its stress on what men can do and on the world as an arena where heroic deeds are possible. The universe inhabited by Santiago, the old Cuban fisherman, is not free of tragedy and pain but these are transcended, and the affirming tone is in sharp contrast with the pessimism permeating such books as *The Sun Also Rises* and *A Farewell to Arms*.

One aspect of this universe, familiar from the earlier works, is its changelessness. The round of Nature—which includes human nature—is not only eternal but eternally the same. The sun not only rises, it rises always, and sets and rises again without change of rhythm. The relationship of Nature to man proceeds through basic patterns that never vary. Therefore, despite the fact that a story by Hemingway is always full of action, the action takes place inside a world that is fundamentally static.

Moreover, its processes are purely secular in character: Hemingway's figures are often religious but their religion is peripheral rather than central to their lives. In *The Old Man and the Sea*, Santiago, the principal figure, is a primitive

Reprinted from Leo Gurko, "The Heroic Impulse in *The Old Man and the Sea*," *English Journal*, October 1955.

Cuban, at once religious and superstitious. Yet neither his religion nor his superstitious beliefs are relevant to his tragic experience with the great marlin; they do not create it or in any way control its meaning. The fisherman himself, knowing what it is all about, relies on his own resources and not on God (in whom he devoutly believes, just as Jake Barnes, while calling himself a bad Catholic, is also a devout believer). If he succeeds in catching the fish he "will say ten Our Fathers and ten Hail Marys . . . and make a pilgrimage to the Virgen de Cobre," but these are rituals that come after the event and have no significant relationship with it.

In this universe, changeless and bare of divinity, everyone has his fixed role to play. Santiago's role is to pursue the great marlin, "That which I was born for," he reflects; the marlin's is to live in the deepest parts of the sea and escape the pursuit of man. The two of them struggle with each other to the death, but without animosity or hatred. On the contrary, the old man feels a deep affection and admiration for the fish. He admires its great strength as it pulls his skiff out to sea, and becomes conscious of its nobility as the two grow closer and closer together, in spirit as well as space, during their long interlude on the Gulf Stream. In the final struggle between them, his hands bleeding, his body racked with fatigue and pain, the old man reflects in his exhaustion:

> You are killing me, fish. . . . But you have a right to. Never have I seen a greater, or more beautiful, or a calmer or a more noble thing than you, brother. Come on and kill me. I do not care who kills who.

On the homeward journey, with the marlin tied to the boat and already under attack from sharks, Santiago establishes his final relationship with the fish, that great phenomenon of Nature:

> You did not kill the fish only to keep alive and to sell for food, he thought. You killed him for pride and because you are a fisherman. You loved him when he was alive and you loved him after. If you love him, it is not a sin to kill him.

A BROTHERHOOD OF NATURE

A sense of brotherhood and love, in a world in which everyone is killing or being killed, binds together the creatures of Nature, establishes between them a unity and an emotion which transcends the destructive pattern in which they are caught. In the eternal round, each living thing, man and animal, acts out its destiny according to the drives of its species, and in the process becomes a part of the profound harmony of the natural universe. This harmony, taking into account the hard facts of pursuit, violence, and death but reaching a stage of feeling beyond them, is a primary aspect of Hemingway's view of the world. Even the sharks have their place. They are largely scavengers, but the strongest and most powerful among them, the great Mako shark which makes its way out of the deep part of the sea, shares the grandeur of the marlin. Santiago kills him but feels identified with him as well:

> But you enjoyed killing the *dentuso*, he thought. He lives on the live fish as you do. He is not a scavenger nor just a moving appetite as some sharks are. He is beautiful and noble and knows no fear of anything.

Nature not only has its own harmony and integration but also its degrees of value. In *The Old Man and the Sea* this is contained in the idea of depth. The deeper the sea the more valuable the creatures living there and the more intense the experience deriving from it. On the day that he catches the great marlin, the old man goes much farther out than the other fishermen and casts bait in much deeper water. The marlin itself is a denizen of the profounder depths. Even the Mako shark lives in the deep water and its speed, power, and directness are qualities associated with depth. There are, in fact, two orders in every species: the great marlins and the lesser, the great sharks and the smaller, bad-smelling, purely scavenger sharks who dwell in shallower water and attack with a sly indirectness in demeaning contrast with the bold approach of the Mako. There are also two kinds of men—as there have always been in Hemingway—the greater men and the lesser, heroes and ordinary humans.

To be a hero means to dare more than other men, to expose oneself to greater dangers, and therefore more greatly to risk the possibilities of defeat and death. On the eighty-fifth day after catching his last fish, Santiago rows far beyond the customary fishing grounds; as he drops his lines into water of unplumbed depth he sees the other fishermen, looking very small, strung out in a line far inland between himself and the shore. Because he is out so far, he catches the great fish. But because the fish is so powerful, it pulls his skiff even farther out—so far from shore then that they cannot get back in time to prevent the marlin being chewed to pieces by the sharks.

"I shouldn't have gone out so far, fish," he said. "Neither for you nor for me. I'm sorry, fish."

A COLLECTIVE AWE

The greatness of the experience and the inevitability of the loss are bound up together. Nature provides us with boundless opportunities for the great experience if we have it in us to respond. The experience carries with it its heavy tragic price. No matter. It is worth it. When Santiago at last returns with the marlin still lashed to the skiff but eaten away to the skeleton, he staggers uphill to his hut groaning under the weight of the mast. He falls asleep exhausted and dreams of the African lions he had seen in his younger days at sea. The next morning the other fishermen gaze in awe at the size of the skeleton, measure it to see by how much it is record-breaking, while the reverential feeling of the boy, Manolin, for the fisherman is strongly reenforced. Everyone has somehow been uplifted by the experience. Even on the lowest, most ignorant level, it creates a sensation. The tourists in the last scene of the story mistake the marlin for a shark but they too are struck by a sense of the extraordinary.

The world not only contains the possibilities of heroic adventure and emotion to which everyone, on whatever level, can respond, but it also has continuity. Santiago is very old and has not much time left. But he has been training Manolin to pick up where he leaves off. The boy has been removed by his parents from the old man's boat because of his bad luck, but this in no way diminishes the boy's eagerness to be like Santiago. The master-pupil relationship between them suggests that the heroic impulse is part of a traditional process handed down from one generation to another, that the world is a continuous skein of possibility and affirmation. This affirming note, subdued in Hemingway's earlier fiction, is sounded here with unambiguous and unrestricted clarity.

A TRUE HERO

Indeed, Santiago is the clearest representation of the hero because he is the only major character in Hemingway who has not been permanently wounded or disillusioned. His heroic side is suggested throughout. Once, in Casablanca, he defeated a huge Negro from Cienfuegos at the hand game and was referred to thereafter as *El Campeón*. Now in his old age, he is hero-worshipped by Manolin who wants al-

THE QUINTESSENTIAL HERO

The *Old Man and the Sea* does give a new definition and meaning to Hemingway's work as a whole. It gives the reader an intensified awareness of how, for Hemingway, the kingdom of Heaven, which is within us, is moral stamina alone, and experience, stripped of illusion, is inexhaustible threat. It is completely clear in this novel, as it is not when his characters are expatriates in Europe, that Hemingway's primary sense of existence is the essential condition of the pioneer. It is above all the terror and isolation of the pioneer in the forest that Hemingway seeks in his prize fighters, matadors, soldiers, and expatriate sportsmen. . . . The giant marlin is a sympathetic character for whom the old man develops a certain fondness and the sharks who destroy all but the marlin's skeleton are villains whom he detests: the astonishing fact remains that one human being is enough to make a genuine narrative. Moreover the old man is not only alone physically, but since he is old he will always be alone, cut off from youth, hope, friendship, love, and all the other relationships which sustain human beings. Hence, as the old man struggles with the sea—with time, nature, and death—he possesses a singular purity of will and emotion. The completeness of his solitude does much to relate the novel to all of Hemingway's work, making one more aware of how some form of solitude isolated every other leading character. . . . Thus, in a way, the old fisherman is the quintessential hero of Hemingway's fiction. Other human beings are simply absent now, and only the sharks are present to interfere with the naked confrontation of man and nature. It is the solitude which requires absolute courage and complete self-reliance.

Delmore Schwartz, *Perspectives USA,* Autumn 1955.

ways to fish with him, or, when he cannot, at least to help him even with his most menial chores. At sea Santiago, sharing the Cuban craze for baseball, thinks frequently of Joe DiMaggio, the greatest ballplayer of his generation, and wonders whether DiMaggio, suffering from a bone spur in his heel, ever endured the pain which the marlin is now subjecting him to. And at night, when he sleeps, he dreams of lions playing on the beaches of Africa. The constant association with the king of ballplayers and the king of beasts adds to the old man's heroic proportions. He is heroic even in his bad luck. The story opens with the announcement that he has gone eighty-four days without taking a fish—ordinary men are seldom afflicted with disaster so outsized.

Heightening and intensifying these already magnified effects is the extraordinary beauty of Nature which cozens and bemuses us with its sensuous intoxications. The account of the sea coming to life at dawn is one of the most moving passages in the story, supplemented later at rhapsodic intervals by the drama of the great pursuit. This comes to its visual climax with the first great jump of the marlin when, for the first time, Santiago sees the gigantic size of his prey. Hemingway pays very close attention to the rippling and fluting of the water, to wind currents, the movements of turtles, fish, and birds, the rising of sun and stars. One is filled not simply with a sense of Nature's vastness, but of her enchantment. This enchantment adds an aesthetic dimension to Santiago's adventure, an adventure whose heroism invests it with moral meaning and whose invocation of comradeship and identity supply it with emotional grandeur.

Within this universe, where there is no limit to the depth of experience, learning how to function is of the greatest importance. It is not enough to have will; one must also have technique. If will is what enables one to live, technique is what enables one to live successfully. Santiago is not a journeyman fisherman, but a superb craftsman who knows his business thoroughly and always practices it with great skill. He keeps his lines straight where others allow them to drift with the current. "It is better to be lucky," he thinks. "But I would rather be exact. Then when luck comes you are ready." To be ready—with all one's professional as well as psychological resources—that is the imperative. One reason that Hemingway's stories are so crammed with technical details about fishing, hunting, bull-fighting, boxing, and war— so much so that they often read like manuals on these subjects—is his belief that professional technique is the quickest and surest way of understanding the physical processes of Nature, of getting into the thing itself. Men should study the world in which they are born as the most serious of all subjects; they can live in it only as they succeed in handling themselves with skill. Life is more than an endurance contest. It is also an art, with rules, rituals, and methods that, once learned, lead on to mastery.

AN INDIVIDUAL FIGHT

Furthermore, when the great trial comes, one must be alone. The pressure and the agony cannot be shared or sloughed off on others, but must be endured alone. Santiago, his hands chafed and bleeding from the pull of the marlin, his face cut, in a state of virtual prostration from his struggle, several times wishes the boy were with him to ease the strain, but it is essential that he go unaccompanied, that in the end he rely on his own resources and endure his trial unaided. At the bottom of this necessity for solitariness, there is the incurable reliance on the individual which makes Hemingway the great contemporary inheritor of the romantic tradition. The stripping down of existence to the struggle between individual man and the natural world, during the course of which he rises to the highest levels of himself, has an early echo in Keats's line "Then on the shore of the wide world I stand alone. . . ." In modern fiction it is Melville and Conrad who give this theme its most significant shape. The mysterious, inscrutable, dramatic Nature into which their heroes plunge themselves in search of their own self-realization supplies Hemingway with the scaffolding for *The Old Man and the Sea.* Like Captain Ahab, like Lord Jim, Santiago is pitched into the dangerous ocean; for only there, and with only himself to fall back on, can he work out his destiny and come to final terms with life.

The concept of the hero whose triumph consists of stretching his own powers to their absolute limits regardless of the physical results gives *The Old Man and the Sea* a special place among its author's works. It confronts us with a man who is not only capable of making the ultimate effort, but makes it successfully and continuously. This theme of affirmation, that had begun to be struck in *Across the River and into the Trees,* is present here much more convincingly. Colonel Cantwell of the immediately preceding novel is forever talking about his heroism; Santiago acts his out. Cantwell reminisces on past triumphs; the old fisherman demonstrates them before our eyes. The strain of boastful exhibitionism that causes some readers to regard Hemingway as an adolescent Byron spoiled Cantwell's story. It is almost totally absent from Santiago's.

Here we have entered a world which has to some degree recovered from the gaping wounds that made it so frightening a place in the early stories. The world which injured Jake Barnes so cruelly, pointlessly deprived Lieutenant Henry of his one love, destroyed Harry Morgan at the height of his powers, and robbed Robert Jordan of his political idealism has now begun to regain its balance. It is no longer the bleak trap within which man is doomed to struggle, suffer, and die as bravely as he can, but a meaningful, integrated structure that challenges our resources, holds forth rich emotional rewards for those who live in it daringly and boldly though continuing to exact heavy payment from them in direct proportion to how far they reach out. There is no less tragedy than before, but this has lost its bleakness and accidentality, and become purposive. It is this sense of purposiveness that makes its first appearance in Hemingway's philosophy, and sets off *The Old Man and the Sea* from his other fiction.

After the first World War the traditional hero disappeared from Western literature, to be replaced in one form or another by Kafka's Mr. K. Hemingway's protagonists, from Nick Adams on, were hemmed in like Mr. K. by a bewildering cosmos which held them in a tight vise. The huge complicated mushrooming of politics, society, and the factory age began to smother freedom of action on the individual's part. In his own life Hemingway tended to avoid the industrialized countries including his own, and was drawn from the start to the primitive places of Spain, Africa, and Cuba. For there, the ancient struggle and harmony between man and Nature still existed, and the heroic possibilities so attractive to Hemingway's temperament had freer play. At last, in the drama of Santiago, a drama entirely outside the framework of modern society and its institutions, he was able to bring these possibilities to their first full fruition, and re-discover, in however specialized a context, the hero lost in the twentieth century.

AN "ENTRY INTO THE NATURAL"

Thus *The Old Man and the Sea* is the culmination of Hemingway's long search for disengagement from the social world and total entry into the natural. This emerges in clearer focus than ever before as one of the major themes in his career both as writer and man. Jake and Bill are happy only in the remote countryside outside Burguete, away from the machinery of postwar Europe. It is when Lieutenant Henry signs his separate peace, deserts from the Italian army, and retires with his love to the high Swiss mountains far removed from the man-made butchery of the war that he enjoys his brief moment of unclouded bliss. The defeated writer in "The Snows of Kilimanjaro," as he lies dying, laments his inability to free himself from the complicated

temptations of money, fashion, the life of sophisticated dilet-
tantism, and thinks of his lost talent as resting unspoiled on
the remote virginal snows cresting the summit of an African
mountain (height on land is plainly the moral equivalent in
Hemingway to depth in the sea). Robert Jordan must first
disengage himself from the political machinery of Spain before the act of sacrificing his life for his comrades can ac-
quire its note of pure spiritual exaltation.

The movement to get out of society and its artifices is not
motivated by the desire to escape but by the desire for liberation. Hemingway seeks to immerse himself totally in Nature not to "evade his responsibilities" but to free his moral
and emotional self. Since life in society is necessarily stunt-
ing and artificial, cowardice consists not of breaking out of
it but of continuing in it. To be true to oneself makes a return
to the lost world of Nature categorically imperative. And that
lost world, as *The Old Man and the Sea* reveals, has its own
responsibilities, disciplines, moralities, and all-embracing
meaning quite the equivalent of anything present in society
and of much greater value because it makes possible a total
response to the demands upon the self. Santiago is the first
of the main figures in Hemingway who is not an American,
and who is altogether free of the entanglements of modern
life. It is toward the creation of such a figure that Hemingway has been moving, however obscurely, from the beginning. His ability to get inside this type of character without
the fatal self-consciousness that mars so much literary
"primitivism" is a measure of how far he has succeeded, in
imagination at least, in freeing himself from the familiar re-
straints of convention.

In this movement from the confinements of society to the
challenges of Nature, Hemingway is most closely linked to
Conrad. Conrad thrust his Europeans into the pressures of the
Malayan archipelago and darkest Africa because he was convinced that only when removed from the comforts and protective mechanisms of civilization could they be put to the
test. In his one London novel, *The Secret Agent*, Conrad
demonstrated that suffering and tragedy were as possible in
Brixton and Camberwell as off the Java coast; heroism, however, was not, and *The Secret Agent* stands as his one major
work that remained hero-less. This embracing of Nature has
nothing of Rousseau in it; it is not a revulsion against the cor-
ruption and iniquity of urban life. It is, instead, a flight from

safety and the atrophying of the spirit produced by safety. It is for the sake of the liberation of the human spirit rather than the purification of social institutions that Conrad and Hemingway play out their lonely dramas in the bosom of Nature.

Because *The Old Man and the Sea* records this drama in its most successful form, it gives off in atmosphere and tone a buoyant sense of release that is new in Hemingway. The story, then, may well be less a capstone of Hemingway's extraordinary career to date than a fresh emotional point of departure for the work to come.

The Old Man Is Not a Heroic Figure

Chaman Nahal

Chaman Nahal is the author of *The Narrative Pattern in Ernest Hemingway's Fiction*, from which the following selection is taken. He has also written a collection of short stories and a book on novelist D.H. Lawrence. Here, Nahal concludes that the old man achieves no heroic victory. In fact, *The Old Man and the Sea* is a tale of resignation, not heroism. Santiago is reconciled to his destiny, and it is in this passivity that he achieves nobility.

An editor of [a book of critical] essays, Katharine T. Jobes, observes in her perceptive introduction: "The disagreement [among critics about *The Old Man and the Sea*] comes in evaluation rather than explication." However, in that disagreement, there is a certain unanimity which is interesting. It lies in the fact that almost all these interpretations of the novel discuss the story as an allegory on an either/or basis. That is, they all see it as two forces pitched against each other. One critic would say it is man against nature. Another, it is the temporal against the eternal. Still another, old age against youth. Another still, heresy against the Christian faith. Thus the divergent interpretations are identical in one respect: they oppose one set of values to another, and see the whole novel as a "fight" between these two sets of values or forces. . . .

My own stand on the novel, as indeed on the rest of Hemingway, is that the work is not a presentation of contention or fight. I have suggested throughout that for Hemingway life existed in plurality and that there was no apparent contradiction for him in that plurality. There is the small life of the individual or any other living creature; and then there is the total life of the universe, which includes and transcends the smaller life of any one particular living organism. The individual no doubt has to pursue his life at his own level. But from time to time he becomes strangely aware of the other, larger life. But there is no inherent "fight" in that awareness. Such moments are rather moments of revelation for him, and come to him when he is in a passive mood. He then goes on with his life in a greater awareness of the total meaning of being alive.

But a part of Hemingway always remained resentful of this vision. Hemingway's intelligence as an artist made him see clearly that the plural nature of the universe could alone explain the life and death cycle to which each living organism is subject. But as a man Hemingway also felt hurt at this vision, for it did not give man the supreme position in the scheme of the universe. What happens in *The Old Man and the Sea* is that Hemingway's resentment against this vision altogether vanishes. Various forms of life are mentioned here, where each form preys on the other for food and life and then in turn becomes a prey to another so that that other life may go on. . . . And in this enormous drama of life, there is no resentment felt by one kind of life against another, nor is there any resentment or bitterness on the part of the novelist who is portraying the play of life for us.

RESIGNATION, NOT VICTORY

The story thus presents a unique theme—the theme of resignation. Santiago is not pitched in battle against anything in the story; there is no either/or survival fight. Consequently there is no victory for man, as most readings of the novel have tried to establish. That this is being said, that the concept of victory is being rejected, does not imply that the contrary concept of "defeat" is being promoted. Such divisive or contradictory terms or ways of thinking split up the beauty of Hemingway's unified vision. If there is no victory for Santiago, moral or physical, there is no defeat either. Santiago neither wins nor loses; he is just resigned to what ultimately does happen to him. He is the purest and the most passive of Hemingway's passive heroes.

That the theme of *The Old Man and the Sea* is resignation, we can understand better if we deal a little more elaborately with the either/or myth. The most obvious of these either/or juxtapositions is man against fate. But in the novel there is no hostile destiny or fate that man has to fight all the time;

fate as an abstract power pitched against man (as in the novels of Thomas Hardy) does not figure here. The same fate that has not given Santiago a fish for eighty-four days has given many to other fishermen; on the very three days that Santiago is wrestling with the marlin, Manolin catches "one the first day. One the second and two the third." Then the same Santiago who is now so unlucky was not always unlucky. His skill in fishing, to which endless references are made, and the accounts he gives of the big fishing done by him earlier, are suggestive of great successes. Like everyone else, he has been lucky on occasions; on other occasions, like the present one, he has been unlucky. In any given moment, fate is kind to some, unkind to others.

Hence, it is not a malicious fate that functions in Hemingway. What is conceived is a power bigger than man, which works according to a set of secret permutations. On the whole it is a benign force, as in one's immediate life it bestows on man many benedictions. But if one tempts it too much, if one asks too much of it, he must be prepared for disappointments. This is what Santiago means when, at the end of the novel, he repeatedly says: "I went too far out." It is not an accusation of a power which is only over there in the "out" and not here in our immediate neighbourhood, as some critics have asserted. For one thing, the old man did not go too far out by choice, he was dragged there by the fish. Secondly, the old man is not for a second afraid of the sea or of a power that may be there too far out. He calls the sea *la mar*—"as feminine and as something that gave or withheld great favours, and if she did wild or wicked things it was because she could not help them." The question of distance does not come into this concept; the sea could be as wicked a foot away from the shore as too far out. Also, the same man who says "I went too far out," has this to say about the distance business: "no man was ever alone on the sea," and "a man is never lost at sea and it is a long island."

A SIMPLE MEANING

So what Santiago means by "I went too far out" (a statement that has been quoted by critics to justify the either/or myth), is that he took too big a risk and hence multiplied his chances of failure. He could have come back successful even from a long trip, to be sure; failure is not implicit in the distance. As it happens, he is coming back as a failure.

Similarly, too much is made of the old man versus the boy allegory. It is true that the old man constantly thinks of the boy while fishing, and he wishes that the boy were there with him: "I wish the boy was here," and "I wish I had the boy." But there is nothing in the story to indicate that the old man resents his age or that these phrases represent a nostalgic longing for his youth. Colonel Cantwell in *Across the River and Into the Trees* resents his age; but not Santiago. He, rather, is vain about his age, for age has taught him tricks which the young do not know. Like the ancient mariner, he thinks of himself as "a strange old man," who has a measure of unbeatable power in him. As he says to the boy: "I may not be as strong as I think, but I know many tricks and I have resolution." Again and again he asserts: "There are plenty of things I can do." And the boy, in the end, tells him the same. He wants to return to the old man, luck or no luck, "for I still have much to learn," and again, "You must get well fast for there is much that I can learn and you can teach me everything."

It is difficult in the face of this evidence to read the novel as an allegory of old age longing for the return of youth. The old man can do without the boy; it is the boy who cannot do without the old man. He is unhappy with the other man, who does not treat him as an equal and will not even let him carry his boat gear. But the old man says to the boy: "I let you carry things when you were five years old." Santiago recalls the memory of the boy very simply because the presence of the boy would be of use to him as additional help. Moreover, the boy was with the old man for the first forty days of the present run of bad luck, and it would be only natural for the old man to think of him out of habit. . . .

ACCEPTANCE OF FATE

It is in Santiago's attitude of resignation that *The Old Man and the Sea* acquires a tremendous magnitude. Santiago is not busy in a fight with nature; he is living his life in terms of acceptance (of things over which he has little control). Not for a moment does it enter the old man's head that he is in any way superior to the rest of life around him; he does not consider himself superior to the fish he has hooked, either. "Man is not much beside the great birds and beasts," says the old man. And whenever he does speak of his superiority to the fish, he does so disparagingly—"I am only better than him through trickery," or "I was only better armed." Throughout the story he calls the fish his "brother," as indeed he calls every other created organism. It is as a part of that vast cosmic drama that the old man takes note of himself; never in pride, only in humility. And it is in that humility that the true glory of the old man lies.

The pain that the old man suffers in the story is not his personal pain; it is rather the pain of the process of being alive. For Hemingway, this pain has been the theme of his entire work. The larger life of the universe is flamboyant and all-powerful. In that larger life, the individual has his own smaller life, which smaller life is itself in some measure an expression of the power and beauty of the larger life of the universe. But in the context of that larger life, the small life of the individual must perforce one day end and is therefore by implication tragic in its scope; hence the pain of that awareness.

The limited pursuit of the old man is the hunt of the fish. Without that he can make no living and would soon starve to death. In that pursuit the old man is shown in absolute mastery of his trade. He is skillful, he keeps his material in readiness, his fishing lines are "straighter" than those of any other fisherman, and most of all he is "exact." He knows the direction of the wind; when he is in a sea current he intuitively "feels" the touch of it on his skiff; he can read his position from the stars; he is "a strange old man" who, in his own words, knows "many tricks," and the boy Manolin is indeed right when he tells him that he has a uniqueness about him unequaled by any fisherman: "There are many good fishermen and some great ones. But there is only you!"

The very physical personality of the old man makes him out to be a uniquely powerful figure and lends him a symbolic grandeur:

> The old man was thin and gaunt with deep wrinkles in the back of his neck. The brown blotches of the benevolent skin cancer the sun brings from its reflection on the tropic sea were on his cheeks. The blotches ran well down the sides of his face and his hands had the deep-creased scars from handling heavy fish on the cords. But none of these scars were fresh. They were as old as erosions in a fishless desert.

Comparisons between *The Old Man and the Sea* and *The Ancient Mariner* have occasionally been made, but it must be seen that there is nothing metaphysical or mysterious about the old man. Nor does Hemingway (unlike Coleridge) bring in the supernatural machinery to create the atmosphere of the tale. The ancient mariner was at the mercy of, indeed was a tool of, supernatural forces. The old man, even in his worst moments, never loses his head. He owes his strength to no one but himself.

Now if there is any "victory" at all for the old man in the novel, it is a victory in the context of the smaller life of the man. The old man cannot bring the fish home, but there is no question that he returns a victor. He may have lost the fish to the sharks, but that is not owing to lack of courage or skill on his part. He gives up only when it is too dark, and when he is left with nothing to carry on the fight; the harpoon, the gaff, the rudder, the oar with the blade are all gone. In the fight with the fish the old man is undoubtedly the winner. But then it is a victory which was never in dispute. The way Hemingway projects the figure of the old man, it was inevitable that he should win against the fish.

However, in the larger life of the universe, the old man definitely suffers a defeat. "'They beat me, Manolin. They truly beat me.'" The "they" of the sentence is the plurality of life that surrounds the old man—the plurality that includes the old man, but also includes the gulf weed, the shrimp, the man-of-war bird, the delicate tern, the schools of bonito and albacore, the tuna and the flying fish, the dolphin, the turtle, the plankton, the warbler, the big marlin, and all the sharks.

It must be repeated that it is not suggested here that the larger life of the universe pursues man with malice or vengeance and imposes a defeat on him in every single encounter. Once the old man had been without a fish for eighty-seven days, but then he caught "big ones every day for three weeks." What is suggested is that these two lives—of the individual and of the universe—run simultaneously, and the individual must be prepared to yield the right of way.

That is precisely what the old man has learned to do in his life—to accept defeat at the hands of the larger life of the universe gracefully and with resignation, and Hemingway in the novel presents a masterly fusion of the two lives or the two modes of living. The old man is conscious of his own power and ability, but he is also conscious of the power and glory of the universe. In resigning himself to the larger life of the universe, the old man does not lose in stature; rather, he rises above the limitations of the smaller life of the individual and acquires heroic proportions. The old man is the most passive of Hemingway's heroes not in the absence of physical power in him or in the will to work. It is because he alone of all his heroes accepts the larger life of the universe without bitterness. He is all-powerful, but he is also all-humble.

It is on this note of humility that the hunt of the great fish begins. For eighty-four days the old man has been without a fish, and with courage and determination he is getting ready to go out once again. The boy cannot go with him—his parents have taken him away from him, regarding the old man as unlucky. But the boy offers the old man a beer, and the old man modestly accepts it. The boy then offers to get fresh sardines for him, to bait the fish with, and also a few baits. Again the old man modestly accepts the offer. And we have these words from Hemingway which go with this moment, describing the mental state of the old man. "He was too simple to wonder when he had attained humility. But he knew he had attained it and he knew it was not disgraceful and it carried no loss of true pride."

Ensues a vast drama on land and the sea, and involving the various creatures that live in the sea. The old man is only an illiterate fisherman, and his awareness of the larger life of the universe has not come to him through knowledge or self-analysis. It has come to him through his passivity, through his humility. As he rows out into the sea, he intuitively thinks in terms of the plurality of things. He knows for certain that the sea "is kind and very beautiful." But he also knows that she can be "so cruel." The sea is also a beloved—"the moon affects her as it does a woman." In this sea live the mighty fish. But there also fly birds that are "so delicate and fine.". . .

And throughout, the old man is completely resigned to the comparative freedom that each living organism has to act, including man. There are absolutely no expressions of *nada* in *The Old Man and the Sea.* There is no bitterness, no denial; there is only acceptance.

The courage that the old man displays is not a defiance of fate or destiny; rather, it is an assertion of the obligation that each man has to himself—it is more an act of duty. When the old man declares, "But man is not made for defeat . . . A man can be destroyed but not defeated," he is not defying his fate. What he means by this is that a man has an obligation to himself to go on in spite of the defeat. He knows very well that a man can be defeated, for he has just been defeated himself and he later admits it to the boy ("They beat me, Manolin. They truly beat me"). But the sentence, "A man can be destroyed but not defeated," is a remarkable expression of the faith of the old man (and of Hemingway) in the dignity of man. What the old man means is that a man can never be defeated out of his will to go on—until he falls. The stress is on dignity, even when the odds are against one. "Take a good rest, small bird. . . . Then go in and take your chance like any man or bird or fish."

The old man is thus utterly reconciled to his destiny and is not only the most passive of Hemingway's heroes, he is the noblest. In the presentation of the story of the old man, Hemingway is able to offer a unified view of the plurality of life that had escaped him earlier.

Chronology

1898

Marcelline Hemingway, Ernest's older sister, born January 15.

1899

Ernest Miller Hemingway born in Oak Park, Illinois, second of six children of Clarence Edmonds Hemingway, M.D., and Grace Hall Hemingway, July 21.

1902

Ursula Hemingway, Ernest's second sister, born April 29.

1904

Madelaine Hemingway, called Sunny, Ernest's third sister, born November 28.

1911

Carol Hemingway, called Beefy or Beefish, Ernest's fourth sister, born July 19.

1914–18

World War I; the United States enters the war in 1917.

1915

Leicester Clarence Hemingway, called Lester de Pester (later shortened to the Pest) by his only brother, Ernest, born April 1.

1917

Graduates from Oak Park High School. Possibly rejected by the army because of an eye injury (received while boxing?). (He may have only assumed he would be rejected, and his bad vision may have predated his attempts at boxing.) Works as a cub reporter for the *Kansas City Star* through April 1918. Eighteenth Amendment to the U.S. Constitution makes alcoholic beverages illegal.

1918

Goes to Italy as a Red Cross ambulance driver. July 8—Severely injured by mortar fragments near Fossalta di Piave, in Italy near the Austrian front. November 11—World War I ends.

1919

Treaty of Versailles.

1920

F. Scott Fitzgerald publishes *This Side of Paradise*. Women are given the right to vote by constitutional amendment. "Red scare" leads to arrest of twenty-seven hundred American Communists.

1920–24

Works as a reporter and foreign correspondent for the *Toronto Star* and *Toronto Star Weekly*.

1921

Marries Hadley Richardson; leaves for Europe.

1921–22

War between Greece and Turkey; Hemingway's first war correspondence in 1922.

1925

Fitzgerald publishes *The Great Gatsby*. Sherwood Anderson publishes *Dark Laughter*.

1926

Hemingway publishes *The Torrents of Spring* (a parody of Anderson's *Dark Laughter*) and *The Sun Also Rises*.

1927

Divorces Hadley Richardson and marries Pauline Pfeiffer.

1928–38

Lives mostly at Key West, Florida.

1929

William Faulkner publishes *The Sound and the Fury*.

1929–37

Great Depression in the United States, following the stock market crash of October 29, 1929.

1933

Eighteenth Amendment repealed (see 1917). President Franklin Roosevelt introduces the "New Deal," programs intended to end the Depression.

1935

Italy invades Ethiopia.

1936–39

Spanish Civil War.

1936–37

Writes, speaks, and raises money for Loyalists in Spanish Civil War.

1937

Japan invades China.

1937–39

In Spain covering civil war for North American Newspaper Alliance.

1938

Germany invades Austria.

1939

John Steinbeck publishes *The Grapes of Wrath.*

1939–45

World War II. The United States enters the war in 1941, after the December 7 Japanese attack on Pearl Harbor.

1940

Pauline Pfeiffer divorces him; he marries Martha Gellhorn.

1941

In China as war correspondent.

1942–45

Covers European theater of war as newspaper and magazine correspondent; also covers war in China, chases submarines in the Caribbean. Establishes Cuban residence in 1942.

1944

August 25—Allied liberation of Paris.

1945

May 7—Germany surrenders. August 15—Japan surrenders after the United States drops atomic bombs on Hiroshima and Nagasaki. World War II ends. December—Divorced from Martha Gellhorn.

1946

Marries Mary Welsh.

1950–53

Korean War; McCarthy era (Senator Joseph McCarthy holds hearings accusing many of being Communists; in 1954 he is condemned for his excesses by the U.S. Senate).

1951

J.D. Salinger publishes *The Catcher in the Rye.*

1952

Ralph Ellison publishes *Invisible Man.*

1953

Awarded the Pulitzer prize for *The Old Man and the Sea.*

1954

Wins Nobel prize for "forceful and style-making mastery of the art of modern narration."

1961

July 2—Dies of self-inflicted gunshot wound in his Ketchum, Idaho, home.

FOR FURTHER RESEARCH

ABOUT ERNEST HEMINGWAY

Matthew J. Bruccoli, ed., *Ernest Hemingway: Cub Reporter.* Pittsburgh: University of Pittsburgh Press, 1970.

Peter Buckley, *Ernest.* New York: Dial Press, 1978.

Anthony Burgess, *Ernest Hemingway and His World.* New York: Charles Scribner's Sons, 1978.

Norberto Fuentes, *Hemingway in Cuba.* Secaucus, NJ: Lyle Stuart, 1984.

Gregory H. Hemingway, *Papa: A Personal Memoir.* Boston: Houghton Mifflin, 1976.

Leicester Hemingway, *My Brother, Ernest Hemingway.* Cleveland: World, 1962.

Mary Welsh Hemingway, *How It Was.* New York: Knopf, 1976.

A.E. Hotchner, *Papa Hemingway: A Personal Memoir.* New York: Random House, 1966.

James R. Mellow, *Hemingway: A Life Without Consequences.* Reading, MA: Addison-Wesley, 1992.

Jeffrey Meyers, *Hemingway: A Biography.* New York: Harper & Row, 1985.

Madelaine Hemingway Miller, *Ernie: Hemingway's Sister Sunny Remembers.* New York: Crown, 1975.

Marcelline Hemingway Sanford, *At the Hemingways: A Family Portrait.* Boston: Atlantic–Little, Brown, 1962.

CRITICAL WORKS ON ERNEST HEMINGWAY

Carlos Baker, ed., *Ernest Hemingway: Critiques of Four Major Novels.* New York: Charles Scribner's Sons, 1962.

——, *Hemingway: The Writer as Artist.* Princeton, NJ: Princeton University Press, 1972.

Sheridan Baker, *Ernest Hemingway: An Introduction and Interpretation*. New York: Holt, Rinehart and Winston, 1967.

Sam S. Baskett, "Toward a 'Fifth Dimension' in *The Old Man and the Sea*," *Centennial Review*, no. 19, 1979.

Jackson J. Benson, *Hemingway: The Writer's Art of Self-Defense*. Minneapolis: University of Minnesota Press, 1969.

Robert Gorham Davis, "Hemingway's Tragic Fisherman," *New York Times Book Review*, September 7, 1952.

Audre Hanneman, *Ernest Hemingway: A Comprehensive Bibliography*. Princeton, NJ: Princeton University Press, 1967.

John Killinger, *Hemingway and the Dead Gods: A Study in Existentialism*. Lexington: University of Kentucky, 1960.

Kelli A. Larson, *Ernest Hemingway: A Reference Guide 1974–1989*. Boston: G.K. Hall, 1991.

Frank Laurence, *Hemingway and the Movies*. Jackson: University of Mississippi, 1981.

Robert Lee, *Ernest Hemingway: New Critical Essays*. Totowa, NJ: Barnes and Noble, 1983.

John McCaffery, *Ernest Hemingway: The Man and His Work*. Cleveland: World, 1950.

Jeffrey Meyers, ed., *Hemingway: The Critical Heritage*. London: Routledge, 1982.

James Nagel, ed., *Ernest Hemingway: The Writer in Context*. Madison: University of Wisconsin Press, 1984.

Chaman Nahal, *The Narrative Pattern in Ernest Hemingway's Fiction*. Rutherford, NJ: Fairleigh Dickinson University Press, 1971.

Mark Schorer, "With Grace Under Pressure," *New Republic*, October 6, 1952.

Robert O. Stephens, *Ernest Hemingway: The Critical Reception*. New York: Burt Franklin, 1977.

Edward R. Stephenson, "The 'Subtle Brotherhood' of Crane and Hemingway," *Hemingway Review*, vol. 1, no. 1, Fall 1981.

Ben Stoltzfus, *Gide and Hemingway: Rebels Against God*. Port Washington, NY: Kennikat, 1978.

Edward Strauch, "*The Old Man and the Sea*: An Anthropological View," *Aligarh Journal of English Studies* 9, 1984.

Linda Welshimer Wagner, ed., *Ernest Hemingway: Six Decades of Criticism.* East Lansing: Michigan State University Press, 1987.

ABOUT ERNEST HEMINGWAY'S TIME

Leon Edel, ed., *The Forties.* New York: Farrar, Straus and Giroux, 1983.

William Wiser, *The Crazy Years: Paris in the Twenties.* New York: Atheneum, 1983.

Peter Wyden, *The Passionate War: The Narrative History of the Spanish Civil War.* New York: Simon & Schuster, 1984.

WORKS BY ERNEST HEMINGWAY

Three Stories and Ten Poems (1923)

in our time (published privately by a small press in Paris) (1924)

In Our Time (first publication by a major American publisher; includes the stories from *Three Stories and Ten Poems*, the sketches from *in our time*, and new stories) (1925)

The Torrents of Spring; The Sun Also Rises (published as *Fiesta* in England) (1926)

Men Without Women (1927)

A Farewell to Arms (1929)

Death in the Afternoon (1932)

Winner Take Nothing (1933)

Green Hills of Africa (1935)

To Have and Have Not (1937)

The Spanish Earth; The Fifth Column and the First Forty-Nine Stories (1938)

For Whom the Bell Tolls (1940)

Men at War (edited by Hemingway) (1942)

Across the River and into the Trees (1950)

The Old Man and the Sea (1952)

PUBLISHED POSTHUMOUSLY

The Wild Years (1962)

A Moveable Feast (1964)

By-Line: Ernest Hemingway (1967)

The Fifth Column and Four Stories of the Spanish Civil War (a new edition of the play and four previously uncollected stories) (1969)

Islands in the Stream (1970)

The Nick Adams Stories (includes some previously unpublished Adams material) (1972)

Complete Poems (1979)

Ernest Hemingway: Selected Letters, 1917–1961, edited by Carlos Baker (1981)

The Dangerous Summer; Dateline: Toronto (1985)

The Garden of Eden (1986)

INDEX

Across the River and Into the Trees,
  28, 54, 55, 83
  on aging, 53
  fable in, 43
Africa, 26
alcoholism, 23
Aldridge, John, 113
allegory, 74, 82
  old age as, 57-58, 160
  see also symbolism/imagery
Anderson, Sherwood, 19
  Hemingway compared with, 22,
  23
Atlantic Monthly, 24

Backman, Melvin, 120
Baker, Carlos, 15, 42, 113, 118, 120,
  122, 123
Barnes, Djuna, 59
baseball, 119
biblical allusions, 69-70, 104-107
Bodhisattva, 32
Boni and Liveright, 22-23
Braden, Spruille, 27
Breit, Harvey, 42, 43
Brumback, Ted, 19
bullfighting
  books about, 21, 25
  compared to fishing, 143
  as religious ceremony, 100-101

Campbell, Joseph, 32, 35, 39
Camus, Albert, 76
Carey, Joyce, 83
Castro, Fidel, 29
characterization
  is fake, 110-13, 114, 116
  realism in, 113, 115
characters
  Manolin, 87, 89
    concern for Santiago, 39, 66-68,
    120, 122, 137-38, 146
    has faith in Santiago, 70
    maturation of, 64-66
    takes care of Santiago, 72, 74

marlin, 34-35
  Christian symbolism of, 97
  cycle of life and death through,
  55-56
  guilt over killing, 36-37
  is deliberately male, 112-13
  is mysterious, 46-47
  Santiago's love/respect for, 92,
  107-108, 148
  Santiago's relationship with, 145
  Santiago's union with, 47, 81, 82,
  94, 123, 142-43
  symbolizes victory, 40
  transcends time, 93
  as work of art, 43, 48
Martin, 70
sea, 81
  femininity of, 88-89
  good and evil of, 34
  power of, 159
  symbolism of, 141
sharks, 36, 37, 38
  realism of, 113-14
  represent reviewers/critics,
  49-50
  symbolize time, 95
tourists, 40, 75, 87, 115, 138
turtles
  objectify journalism, 50-51
  see also Santiago
Collier's magazine, 27
Connable, Harriet, 18
Connable, Ralph, 18
Conrad, Joseph, 155-56
Cooperman, Stanley, 52, 74
Cranston, J. Herbert, 21
Crook Factory, 27, 28
Cuba, 26, 27, 29-30

Dark Laughter (Anderson), 23
death, 76-77, 82, 86
  and manhood, 101-102
  rebirth through, 93-94
Death in the Afternoon, 16, 21, 25,
  99, 140

depression, 26, 30
diabetes, 24, 30
Dial magazine, 20, 22
dialogue, 61-63
  see also narration
DiMaggio, Joe, 41, 81, 84–85, 119, 151
Dunn, Gordon E., 111

Eliot, T.S., 59
Elliot, Gary D., 133
Esquire (magazine), 26, 79, 111
existentialism, 73, 77, 125–26

Farewell to Arms, A, 16–17, 55, 106, 115
  pessimism in, 147
Faulkner, William, 46, 66, 110
Fifth Column and the First Forty-Nine Stories, The, 27
Finca Vigía, 27
Flora, Joseph M., 104
For Whom the Bell Tolls, 27, 55, 83
  language in, 60
France
  Hemingway lives in, 19–20, 22, 24
  Hemingway travels in, 21, 26

Galantière, Lewis, 19–20
Gellhorn, Martha (wife), 27–28
Gifford, William, 74
Greco-Turkish War, 20–21
Green Hills of Africa, 26, 134
Gurko, Leo, 147

Halverson, John, 72
Handy, William J., 75, 128-38
Harada, Keiichi, 88
Heart of Darkness (Conrad)
  Santiago compared to Kurtz, 82
Hemingway, Alfred Tyler, 15
Hemingway, Bumby, 21, 25
Hemingway, Clarence, 13–14, 18, 19
  suicide of, 24–25
Hemingway, Ernest, 16
  on aging, 52–54, 58
  childhood of, 14–15
  children of, 21, 24, 25
  and fishing, 79–80
  fiction of
    exemplary heroes in, 86-87
    fable in, 36, 114-15, 154-55
    God and manhood in, 98–100, 109
    realism in, 114-15
  journalism career of, 15–16, 19–21
  parents of, 13–14
    disappoints, 18-19, 23-24
  prizes won by, 29
  as Santiago, 43–44, 48, 51

and Shakespeare, 63, 114
suicide of, 30
travels of, 21, 26, 29
and William Faulkner, 46, 66, 110
in World War II, 16-17
writing career of, 22–23, 28-29
Hemingway, Grace Hall (mother), 13–15, 18, 19, 21, 23
Hemingway, Gregory Hancock (son), 25
Hemingway, John Hadley Nicanor.
  See Hemingway, Bumby
Hemingway, Leicester (brother), 25
Hemingway, Marcelline (sister), 14–15, 17
Hemingway, Patrick (son), 24
Hemingway, Sunny (sister), 19
Hemingway, Ursula (sister), 19
Hemingway and the Dead Gods (Killinger), 77
Hofling, Charles K., 70-71
Huckleberry Finn (Twain), 138

imagery. *See* symbolism/imagery
Imagist doctrine, 59-60
In Our Time, 17, 22–23
irony, 40, 41
Italian Silver Medal, 17
Italy
  Hemingway at war in, 16–17
  Hemingway travels in, 20

Jobes, Katharine T., 157

Kafka, Franz, 154
Kansas City Star, 15–16
Keats, John, 114
Key West, Florida, 24–25, 27
Killers, The, 64
Killinger, John, 72, 77

LaMonte, Francesca, 112
language. *See* narration
Lanham, General, 83
Levin, Harry, 52
Life (magazine), 28–29
Little Review, 20
Lovejoy, A.O., 140
Lynn, Kenneth S., 13, 17, 24

manhood
  achieving, 55
  vs. brotherhood, 56-57
  failure of, 54
  God and, 98–100
  Hemingway's philosophy on, 100-102
  and defeat in, 73–74
Mayo Clinic, 30
McAlmon, Robert, 21

Mellow, James, 22
Men Without Women, 24
Meyerhoff, Hans, 93
Moby-Dick (Melville)
  Santiago compared with Ahab in,
    35, 76, 82, 135, 153
Mussolini, Benito, 21
mythology, 33

Nahal, Chaman, 157
narration, 64–66
  flaws in, 84–85
  poetry in, 83–84
  simplicity in, 60–61
  see also dialogue
"Natural History of the Dead, A," 16
nature, 152
  good and evil in, 34, 38
  humbles Santiago, 81
  mans union with, 148–50, 154–56
  Santiago is at one with, 82, 87
  Santiago rebels against, 71–72
Nobel Prize, 29
North American Newspaper Alliance (NANA), 26–27

Old Man and the Sea, The,
  as allegory, 42, 57-58, 160
  autobiographical elements in,
    43–44, 48, 50–51
  compared with *Huckleberry Finn,*
    138
  different levels of reading in,
    96–97, 98
  as fable, 32–33, 36, 43
  first published, 29
  flaws in
    characterization, 109–13
    narration, 84–85
    style, 116
  as folk tale, 83
  Imagist doctrine in, 59–60
  interpretations of, 42–43, 118, 157
  is expanded from Hemingway's
    essay, 79–80
  realism in, 113, 115
  see also characters; narration;
    style; symbolism/imagery;
    themes
Oldsey, Bernard S., 73
"On the Blue Water," 111

Paris Review, 139
Perkins, Maxwell, 15, 23, 26, 28
Pfeiffer, Gus, 24
Pfeiffer, Pauline, 23, 24, 27
Pilar (ship), 26, 27
Plimpton, George, 139
PM (periodical), 27
Pound, Ezra, 19, 20

Pulitzer Prize, 29

Richardson, Elizabeth Hadley
  (wife), 19
  divorce from Hemingway, 23
  pregnancy of, 21
Rime of the Ancient Mariner, The
  (Coleridge), 161–62
Rovit, Earl, 33, 35

Santiago, 69–70
  as artist, 43-44, 45-47, 50-51
  as autobiographical, 43–44, 48
  as central and changing image,
    133–37
  characterization of, is fake,
    110–13
  as Christ figure, 69–70, 71–72, 97,
    106-107, 145-46
  and fighter code, 120-21
  Hemingway's idea of, 72, 75
  vs. pagan, 77
  is defeated
    acceptance of, 160, 162-64
    cannot be, 73–74
    and fighter code, 123-24, 125-26
    as quest hero, 39–40
  determination of, 92–93
  doubts his actions, 35–38
  guides Manolin into manhood,
    64–65
  heroism of, 150–52
  injured pride of, 74–75
  isolation of, 44-45, 89, 153
  and love, 107–108
  and old age, 56
    allegory for, 57-58
    does not resent, 160
  pride of , 40-41
    injured, 74-75
    and humility, 55, 76, 80–83, 119,
      121–22
    vs. outward appearance, 69-71
  protests mortality, 76-77
  as "quest" hero, 32–33, 94
  for the community, 34
  relationship with Manolin, 40,
    150-51, 160
    love between, 59, 62-63, 66-68
    shared faith through, 107
  religion of, 124–25, 147–48
  and society, 35, 37–38, 86–87
  speech of, 60
  as spiritually fulfilled, 129–31, 133
    true existence and love through,
      131–32
Schorer, Mark, 36, 42, 43, 81
Schwartz, Delmore, 151
Scribner's, 23, 24
Secret Agent, The (Conrad), 155

setting, 66, 134
sea in, 141
Shakespeare, William, 114
"The Short Happy Life of Francis Macomber," 26
Sino-Japanese War, 27
Snows of Kilimanjaro, The, 26, 52, 90, 128–29
Spain
  Hemingway travels in, 21, 25, 26–27, 29
Spanish Civil War, 26–27
Spector, Robert Donald, 64, 65
Stein, Gertrude, 19, 20, 22
Stephens, Robert O., 139
Steward, Don, 22
Stoltzfus, Ben, 69
style
  dream vs. experience, 90
  "iceberg," 139
  is too chummy, 116–17
suicide
  of Ernest Hemingway, 30
  of Hemingway's father, 24–25
Sun Also Rises, The, 20, 23, 24, 101
  language in, 60
  pessimism in, 147
Switzerland, 21
symbolism/imagery, 84
  bird, 34
  Christ figure, 69-70, 71, 97, 106-107, 145-46
  does not exist, 67
  and fighter code, 120-21
  is Hemingway's idea, 72, 75
  Christian, 47, 97–98, 146
    vs. humanism, 85–86
    superficial, 102–103
    see also biblical allusions
  eyes, 70
  fish, 39, 47
  fishing "far out," 94–95, 104–105
  Joe DiMaggio, 90–92, 93, 107, 119, 151
  lions, 48–49, 90, 93, 107, 127
  marlin, 93–94
  mast, 67, 72
  men fighting beasts, 143-44
  Santiago, as willed creation, 57
  sea, 88–89, 141–42
  sharks, 49–50, 94–95, 141-42
  swimming against the current, 73
  see also themes

themes
  aging, 52–54, 58
  and fear of passivity, 54–55
  art/artist allegory, 42, 43, 45–46
    and criticism, 49
    and the masterpiece, 47–48

mystery in, 46–47
  choice, 142-43
  fighter code, 119–20
    and Christ, 120–21, 122
    and sin, 124-25
  individual and society, 157–58, 161
  inner pride vs. outer failure, 69–71
  inner success vs. outer success, 130–32
  isolation, 44–45, 74, 87, 89, 152–53
    and manhood, 99–100
    and Santiago's truth, 56–57
  killing, as sin, 37, 124–25
    vs. hubris, 94–95
  love, 107–108
    between Santiago and Manolin, 59, 62, 66–68
  man
    as invincible, 73-74
    as transcending animal nature, 139–41, 143–45
  manhood, 98–102
  power of will, 54, 55–56
  process of living and dying, 82
  rebellion against God, 69, 72
  resignation, 158–59, 160, 162–64
  see also symbolism/imagery, Christ figure
Three Stories and Ten Poems, 21
Toklas, Alice B., 20
Toronto Star Weekly, 18, 20
Torrents of Spring, The, 23, 27
Tracy, Spencer, 29
tragedy, 42–43
  Christian, 49, 51

"Undefeated, The," 96, 99–100, 101, 140

"Very Short Story, A," 17
von Kurowsky, Agnes, 17, 18
Voss, Gilbert, 112, 114

Wagner, Linda, 59
Waldhorn, Arthur, 79
Waldmeir, Joseph, 96
Weekly Star, 21
Weeks, Robert P., 109
Wellington, C.G., 16
Welsh, Mary (wife), 28, 29, 30
Williams, Wirt, 42
Wilson, Edmund, 22
Windemere, 15, 18, 19
Winner Take Nothing, 26
Wittkowski, Wolfgang, 118
World War II, 27–28
Wylder, Delbert, 32

Young, Philip, 42–43, 82, 118